⁚Photographing Nature⁚

PHOTOGRAPHING
NATURE

David Linton

GEORGE G. HARRAP & CO. LTD
London · Toronto · Wellington · Sydney

PUBLISHER'S NOTE

All the equipment and materials mentioned in this
book are available in Great Britain.
Modifications to the American spelling and idiom have
been limited to those considered necessary to present
the text in a more familiar form.

The line illustrations for this book were prepared by
the Graphic Arts Division of The American Museum
of Natural History. The photographs are by the author,
unless otherwise indicated.

First published in Great Britain 1965
by GEORGE G. HARRAP & CO. LTD
182 High Holborn, London W.C.1
© *David Linton* 1960, 1961, 1962, 1963, 1965

Composed in Monotype Imprint and printed by
The Whitefriars Press Limited, London and Tonbridge.
Made in Great Britain

To my wife Ann
who has a way with wild creatures,
including young *Homo sapiens*

Contents:

PART TWO: APPLICATIONS

List of Illustrations:

List of Plates:

Introduction:

IT is not altogether a coincidence that interest in nature photography has grown at the same time that nature itself has become increasingly remote from the lives of most people. The audience for films and books on nature subjects has never before been so large or so attentive, and with the rapid expansion of leisure and the increasing interest in recreation of all sorts that are the most outstanding features of life in the second half of the twentieth century, it is inevitable that to photograph nature has become, instead of the preserve of a select few, a rewarding avocation for many.

Nature photography does not differ significantly in technique from other kinds of photography; the difference is in the photographer's approach. Nature photography demands a respectful appreciation of things as God made them—a quality that illuminates much of the best photography in other fields as well. The photographer does not create a nature picture, he reveals it. He must learn to avoid anthropomorphism, the tendency to attribute human qualities and attitudes to non-human subjects, which is seen at its worst on television and in the movies.

This book is not divided by subjects—Birds, Flowers, Mammals, and so on—because such a scheme causes much of the photographic information to be needlessly repeated. It is assumed that the reader is already familiar with simple, general photography and its vocabulary. The material about photography, which applies to any subject matter, has been covered only once, in Part One. Specific applications of these fundamentals, and particularly those that involve unusual problems, are discussed in Part Two. In Chapter 14 and in the Bibliography are trail signs for those who would like to go farther.

Readers may note that the plates are not accompanied by the conventional technical data—shutter speeds, aperture, type of film, make of camera, etc. There are several reasons for this. During 1948, the first year that I took pictures every day, I read photographic books and magazines avidly and, emulating them, I kept a record of these items. I soon found, however, that the paper work interfered seriously with my picture taking. A little later I realized that I did not actually use any of this information, and that it was, in fact, quite useless. Information on exposure means very little unless it is considered in relation to the intensity, contrast, and quality of the light. In nature, these things are constantly changing.

Those who read on in this book will find that I do not think the type of film or make of camera used has much effect on the resulting picture. Most active professional photographers use a variety of cameras; often they do not remember which one was used for a certain picture. The choice is chiefly a matter of convenience. In Antarctica in 1962, for example, I used 35-mm. equipment exlusively, simply because there are no photographic supply shops there and I had to keep the weight of my outfit to a minimum. I therefore standardized on one size of film. If I were to take some of those same pictures in the studio I would use a large view camera because it is permanently set up in the studio and with the darkroom next door it is easy to develop individual sheets of film to check the results. The plates in this book were made with various cameras, including all the different types described in Chapter 2. Where there are technical points that seem relevant they are mentioned in the captions.

Parts of this book have appeared in *Natural History* magazine. Special thanks are due to Hubert C. Birnbaum, associate editor of that magazine, for his thoughtful editing of those articles as well as his helpful comments on the rest of the manuscript. I am also indebted to Marty Forscher of Professional Camera Repair Service and to Anne Hessey for reviewing and commenting on the text, and to my wife for putting up with all the inconveniences attendant upon its creation and for typing the final result.

D. L.

Part One

FUNDAMENTALS

I :

The Open Eye

WHAT is the most important thing to have in order to take good pictures? Is it a fine camera with fast lenses and extensive lighting apparatus? Apparently not, because we have seen many fine pictures taken with the simplest equipment (witness Arnold Genthe's coverage of the San Francisco fire, done with a borrowed box camera). Would it be a thorough understanding of the fundamentals of photographic technique? No—or most of the good pictures we see around us wouldn't exist.

I think the first requirement is *an open eye*—the ability to *see* pictures. That is the essence of all photography, and particularly of nature photography. I think we should be less concerned with the wide aperture of the lens and more concerned with keeping a wide-open eye behind it.

The chief reason for learning photographic technique is to be freed from it—to keep it out of the way so we can concentrate on what we see. In fact, ignorance of technique is sometimes a blessing. We have all seen exciting pictures made by beginning photographers with no understanding of the fundamentals and no real experience. Although this fact is most disconcerting to experienced photographers, it is undeniable.

Some of the liveliest pictures ever taken were made in the very early years of photography, using techniques and equipment that would make us turn and run today. Why did the mid-nineteenth-century English photographers like Julia Margaret Cameron and David Octavius Hill or their French and American contemporaries produce such a remarkably high proportion of good pictures? One explanation that has often been advanced is that most of them had art training before they took up photography. This explanation, however, doesn't help much—we find lots of photographers with art training today and they're just about the same as the rest of us.

It has also been suggested that the very difficulty of the new medium made the early photographers work harder. That is certainly true. After William Henry Jackson, the expedition photographer whose pictures helped to induce the U.S. Congress to establish Yellowstone National Park and thus found the National Park system, had scrambled up a mountain with his 20 × 24-inch camera, a wooden case of glass plates, a stove, chemicals, and a portable darkroom tent; when he had set all this up on some wind-swept pinnacle, heated and mixed the emulsion and coated the plates with it, then rushed the wet plate to the camera in a light-tight box, he was not inclined, I am sure, to take photography lightly.

But whether this explains the results Jackson got is another question, and a moot one. We do not find that pictures taken now with great difficulty are noticeably better than those that are easy to take. If anything, they are worse.

I think there must be another reason. The early photographers did not have their memories cluttered with pictures. Of course, they had studied paintings and drawings, but the quantity was negligible compared to the deluge of pictures that engulfs us today. Inflation had not yet undermined the value of images. Their minds and eyes were open. They didn't know what was technically possible and impossible, but they wanted to find out, and that challenge helped them produce pictures that are memorable still, after all these years.

Today, very little is really 'impossible' to photograph. We can now photograph anything that can be seen, and a lot that can't. But technical progress has not found us ready with corresponding progress in our thinking about what a picture should be. Instead of opening up ways of doing new things, the vastly improved tools have often simply made it easier for us to do the same old things less well. In just the same way, the invention of the flash bulb ushered in a 20-year period of stagnation in newspaper photography. At a time when 'getting the picture' was the only requirement, taking pictures suddenly became so easy that a chimpanzee could learn to do it, and there was then no effective challenge to the press photographers' thinking. The dark ages are now past in that branch of the field, and the creative intelligence of newspaper photographers has been channelled toward the *content* of pictures rather than the means of taking them.

Photography is something like Antaeus, the giant with whom Hercules wrestled. He was invincible as long as he touched his mother, Earth, and Hercules fought a losing battle until he lifted Antaeus off his feet. So photography must touch home base—the real world—to keep its strength. No photographer, no matter how brilliant, can invent better pictures than nature creates. Our problem is to find them, isolate them, and fit them into the small compass of what we call a picture.

The biggest obstacle to this endeavour is the preconceived idea. No two events in nature are ever exactly alike, but all of us have seen so many pictures that when we go to photograph something we are likely to start out with an already-formed idea of what it should look like. When we get there and find that it does not look like our mind's-eye view we're likely to be disappointed and miss the real picture.

Planning a picture in advance is good, but not when it replaces seeing. The picture of the two fishermen in a dory (see Plate 5) is an example. It was part of a picture story on a Newfoundland fisherman and his family. One picture of men fishing was absolutely essential to the story, but most of the time I was at the fishermen's remote village the weather was so bad that the boats stayed on shore. On the one day that looked promising, I got up before dawn and went out with two boatloads of fishermen. The fog was so heavy that they could not find the fishing grounds. Rain drenched my cameras and I was frightfully seasick. After catching nothing for a couple of hours, the fishermen turned back. I had only a few pictures, and was sure the story was ruined. But this one picture actually told the story better than a well-lighted shot with the boat full of fish. Eventually it became one of my favourites.

Every photographer has had the unsettling experience of finding relevant, important elements in his pictures that he did not notice when he took them. I say 'notice' because there is no doubt that they were seen, but the photographer's reaction was so quick and instinctive that the conscious mind never got into the act. These 'accidents' are not accidental at all; they are simply another indication of the vast, often untapped, resources of the human mind. They are of the same stuff as the sudden, original insights which are so often crucial in scientific discovery; the unconscious synthesis of years of training, study, and practice.

One of the most memorable pictures of the Vanguard rocket that blew up on the pad was taken by the American magazine photographer Burt Glinn. In the foreground, forming a perfect frame for the conflagration, are four pelicans, obviously frightened into flight by the noise of their flightless neighbour. As Glinn tells the story, he shipped the film off to the laboratory and waited nervously for the report. The next day he got it by phone: 'The picture is good and the birds are just wonderful.' His answer was, 'What birds?'

This has happened to me perhaps a dozen times. Not long ago I was photographing a busy street from a second-floor window. As I squeezed the shutter a curious and quite irrelevant thought entered my mind. I remembered a story I had heard a couple of years back. It concerned a man who went to the opening of a Broadway play. During the first act he noticed that the seat next to him was occupied by a dog, who sat up and watched the action on the stage with great interest. At the end of the act, the dog applauded vigorously. As the house lights came on, the man turned to the dog's human companion and said, 'I don't understand. He seems to be following the play and enjoying every minute of it. Is that possible?'

'I can't understand it either,' said the companion. 'He didn't like the book at all.'

I was completely at a loss to understand why this story came so forcefully to mind while I was photographing a city street. But later, when I examined an enlargement of the picture, I found the answer. Someone had left a dog in one of the parked cars on the other side of the street. The dog, sitting in the driver's seat with its paws on the steering wheel, seemed to be about to drive away.

There is probably a certain unconscious element in every good picture. There has to be, because there are so many facets to most pictures that the conscious mind could hardly encompass them all at the moment of exposure, yet they all fall into a perfect relationship so frequently that it cannot be accidental. The open mind—the open eye—can respond to them and organize them into a picture. The mind limited by preconceived images cannot.

2.

Camera Equipment

NATURE photographs can be made with almost any kind of equipment, but some types are more convenient than others. The choice should depend on the field of nature photography that most interests the photographer. And it should be remembered that an expensive camera is not a better choice than an inexpensive one unless the features that make it expensive are used.

There are four basic types of cameras in general use today; each has advantages and disadvantages. There are variations of each of them, and there are some cameras that are intermediate between basic types.

The view camera—a convenient generic term to cover studio, field, plate, technical, monorail, and similar equipment—is one in which the image can be examined and focused directly on a ground glass. The range-finder camera uses a separate optical device to measure the distance to the subject. In the single-lens reflex camera, the image is examined indirectly in a mirror. The twin-lens reflex uses two lenses, one to take the picture and another to project an image for viewing and focusing. Each of these types is discussed in more detail below.

There is, of course, a fifth type of camera that has no built-in focusing system at all. Good pictures can be made with them, but their usefulness is limited. The late Alfred Stieglitz, eminent American photographer and proponent of photography as a fine art, is said to have remarked that no one had exhausted the creative possibilities of the box camera. Whether or not he said it, it is a sound observation. Generally, an inexpensive camera that you know how to use is better than an expensive one of which you are unsure. There is a widespread belief among neophytes that expensive cameras are complicated while inexpensive ones are simple. This idea probably stems from comparisons of box cameras with cameras on which the shutter speed and aperture can be changed, and lives on because it is comforting to believe that something one cannot afford has great disadvantages. Actually, good equipment, whether expensive or not, is simple to use, although the mechanism inside may be complex.

Rapidity of operation is one of the few ways in which the type of camera used has any relevance to the results achieved. Consider this example. In the single-lens reflex class of cameras the better models have automatic diaphragms and mirrors. With these cameras the change from viewing condition to picture-taking condition and back again is accomplished by one squeeze of the trigger. With many less expensive single-lens reflex cameras the diaphragm must be closed by turning a ring on the lens mount before the picture is taken; it must be re-opened after the exposure by turning the ring back again, and the mirror must be returned to viewing position by winding the film advance. How could anyone describe such a sequence as 'simple'?

The automatic features of the more expensive single-lens reflex actually make it capable of photographing events that happen too quickly to be caught by the manually operated camera. A range-finder camera, in turn, would have the same advantage over one with ground-glass focusing.

To judge from those I have met, inexperienced photographers are more likely to have too many features on their cameras than too few. This is doubtless due partly to simple inexperience and the uncritical acceptance of advertising claims, but the main cause is the use of cameras for non-photographic purposes—as status symbols.

Lens and Film Considerations

The most common waste of money is on fast lenses (see Chapter 3). Manufacturers have found that the public thinks fast lenses are better than slow ones, and they have done nothing to correct this misapprehension. In reality, a high-speed lens, like any other feature, is valuable only if you need it. It is a liability if you don't, because something has to be compromised in the lens design to achieve the high speed. Usually it is the sharpness at small apertures that suffers. (One of the first high-speed lenses for 35-mm. cameras was made so that it could not be stopped down beyond $f/11$ because in pre-production tests the image fell apart at smaller apertures.) Advances in lens design and manufacture since World War II have brought improvements in speed, resolution, and the various optical corrections so that some fast lenses are now better than some slow ones, simply because they are newer.

If you have been taking pictures for some time, there is a simple test that will tell whether you need a faster lens: estimate the percentage of pictures you have taken at the maximum aperture of your present lens. Then estimate the percentage of pictures for which you would have used a larger aperture had one been available. If either of these figures is large enough to notice, your experience is exceptional and the purchase of a faster lens is justified.

How should one go about choosing a camera? By deciding first what kind of work is most important to him and then selecting the camera that will do that kind of work best from among those he can afford. Most cameras can do most kinds of work acceptably, but one that is properly chosen for the job may be so much more convenient that it actually increases the range of possible pictures.

Cameras can be classified by the shape of film they use or by their system of focusing. Film comes in sheets, in short rolls with or without a paper backing (called 'roll film'), and in longer rolls without backing paper (usually called 'miniature films'). The last type is usually encountered in the form of 35-mm. film although some specialized cameras use the same sort of film in 70-mm. or $3\frac{1}{2}$-inch widths.

The types of film differ in more than shape. The emulsions are different—even when they have the same name—and so is the base, or supporting material. There exists a hybrid stock called film pack, which is roll film cut into sheets and attached to short strips of backing paper. It is so annoying to shoot, process, and print from that it can best be ignored.

The advantages once claimed for large film sizes have been eliminated by modern emulsions, which make it quite possible to obtain any desired negative characteristic on any size of film. Film size, therefore, is not a consideration in itself. Other factors, such as the availability of certain emulsions or the ease with which certain manipulations can be performed may, however, point to one or another size for certain uses. For example, High Speed Infra-red film is not available in sheet sizes, nor orthochromatic (not sensitive to red) material in rolls. Only continuous films, such as 35-mm. or 70-mm. stock, are practical when a large number of pictures are to be taken by a remotely-controlled or automatic unattended camera. Polaroid 'instant image' film is very useful for making test exposures for immediate examination before the final picture is made. This film can be substituted for the regular film only in sheet-film cameras for which adaptor backs are available. For some kinds of work (obviously involving subjects that do not move) the availability of this material is a compelling consideration in favour of the large camera.

View Cameras: Swings and Tilts

Characteristics of the camera itself may make it appropriate for certain types of work. Only the view camera has adjustments, called 'swings and tilts,' for rendering parallel lines parallel and controlling perspective. It is consequently the first choice for architectural photography, still lifes, small objects, and some more technical uses. Among the view camera's other unique attributes is the ability to change its apparent viewpoint without actually being moved, i.e., within limits it can take a picture that appears to have been taken from a point higher, lower, or more to either side than the actual camera location. These special capabilities recommend the view camera for landscapes wherever its size and weight are not too great a disadvantage.

This is the one type of camera that can be used successfully to solve the common problem of photographing a building or tree from ground level. In order to get the top of the subject in the picture, a photographer using any camera other than a view camera must tip the camera upward. But when he does so the subject appears to lean backward. The correct solution is possible only with a camera on which the front and back can be 'swung' (rotated on horizontal or vertical axes) or 'slid' (moved laterally or up and down). These movements, once the photographer learns how to use them, give the view camera great accuracy as a recording instrument and great flexibility as a creative tool.

Of course, for these controls to be used the camera must be

mounted on a fixed support (usually a tripod) and it must have a ground-glass screen on which the entire image can be seen. Consequently, this type of camera is really practical only in large film sizes—4 × 5 inches and up—in which the available films are in sheet form and require film holders. These factors combine to make the view camera large, heavy, and slow to operate, but it provides unmatched image control.

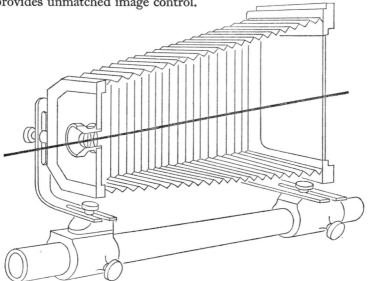

Fig. 1 A view camera, in this case a monorail type.

The Press Camera

Cameras that take sheet film but do not have swings and tilts no longer provide any advantages and are fast becoming obsolete. The 'press' camera belongs to the era of the illiterate reporter with his cigar and braces, his turned-up hat brim, and the press card stuck in his hat; in short, it belongs in *The Front Page*. It was designed to meet two needs: to provide fast shutter speeds at a time when the 'window blind' type of focal-plane shutter was the only way of achieving them, and to utilize the first flash bulb, which was the size of a 100-watt bulb. Today even press photographers have largely abandoned the press camera in favour of lighter and more adaptable equipment.

Incidentally, the press camera of pre-flash-bulb days, when press photographers wore top hats and tails, was a $3\frac{1}{4} \times 4\frac{1}{4}$-inch Graflex with a $6\frac{1}{2}$-inch Taylor Hobson Cooke lens that boasted the astonishingly fast aperture of $f/2.5$! There are a few of these cameras still operating and they have enjoyed quite a vogue recently among fashion and advertising photographers. The delicate unsharpness of the pictures they produce is right in style!

The one advantage of the press camera is its sturdiness. There isn't much mechanism to get out of order. It is the best choice for photographing riots because after the photographer has used up his film he can use the camera as a weapon to fight his way out. The chances are that the camera won't even be damaged.

The 'miniature press' camera (smaller than 4×5 inches) is about as useful as a miniature printing press. There are also some cameras in a limbo between the press and view categories. They usually claim to be both, but they have the advantages of neither. A camera cannot function like a view camera if it is enclosed in a press camera's rigid box—the box gets in the way of the swings. The only notable advantage of such cameras is that, like press cameras, they are sturdy.

The cameras we have discussed are designed to use sheet film or plates; adaptors permit the use of roll film in some of them. Some also have range finders, but the primary method of focusing is by a ground-glass screen mounted in the focal plane and examined directly, sometimes with the aid of a small magnifier. After the image is in focus the ground glass is moved out of the way and its place is taken by the film, encased in a holder. This system of focusing is generally impractical in small sizes because the photographer cannot see a small image clearly enough to focus precisely. It is used, however, with a magnifier in some copying devices that use small film.

Reflex and Range-finder Cameras

Smaller cameras use reflex or range-finder focusing. Reflex focusing uses a ground glass which, instead of being in the same place that is later occupied by the film, is at exactly the same distance from the lens but in a different position. In the single-lens reflex camera, a mirror diverts the image from the film plane to the ground glass. The twin-lens reflex uses one lens to take the picture and another to project an image on the ground glass.

The range-finder camera has a separate optical device to measure the distance from camera to subject, and uses this information to focus the camera through a mechanical coupling to the lens. The range finder works by juxtaposing the images 'seen' through two windows a few inches apart. The apparatus is adjusted until the two images coincide; the angle between the two lines of sight then

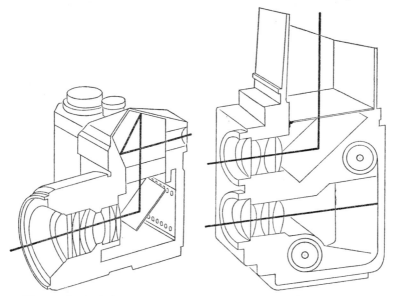

Fig. 2 A single-lens reflex camera, free from parallax, small image; and, right, *a twin-lens reflex camera, parallax, but four-times larger image.*

indicates the distance to the subject. This is basically the same mechanism that gives depth perception to humans and other animals having two eyes that see the same scene from different angles (vision uses other mechanisms in addition).

Some reflex cameras have a prismatic 'range-finder spot' in the ground glass, on which the image appears split or disrupted when it is out of focus, becoming whole and well defined when the focus is sharp. This is not really a range finder but a magnifying device to show more clearly when the ground-glass image is in focus.

It is sometimes useful, but usually less so than the purchasers of the cameras expect. The spot often 'blacks out' at low light levels, when used with slow or very long lenses, or for extreme close-ups. The latter two situations are precisely those for which the single-lens reflex camera is best adapted, so the range-finder spot should not be taken too seriously as a selling point. Certainly any camera that has one should also be provided with a plain ground glass that can be substituted for the one with the spot. There is, incidentally, one camera on the market, the Alpa 8b, that has a genuine range

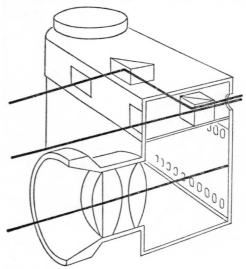

Fig. 3 A range-finder camera shoots quickly, is compact and lightweight.

finder in addition to, but completely separate from, its regular reflex viewing system. It succeeds in preserving most of the virtues of both systems.

Advantages and Disadvantages

The advantages and disadvantages of the three types of small cameras may be summarized as follows:

The twin-lens reflex is the best choice for the beginner. It is the camera to get if you photograph all sorts of subjects and can have only one camera and no extra lenses. The viewing system makes it very easy to see what is included in the picture. Each negative is four times the size of 35 mm. and costs only one-and-a-half times as much.

The image on the ground glass is reversed from left to right, which may be quite disturbing when one is trying to follow a moving subject. Accessory eye-level viewers may be attached to some twin-lens reflexes to provide an unreversed image. The twin-lens reflex is convenient at moderate distances and for medium-sized subjects, such as people. It is not a good choice for extreme close-ups because of parallax—the difference in viewpoint between the viewing and taking lenses. Because there are two lenses coupled together, to change lenses on this type of camera necessitates interchangeable lens panels, as introduced by Mamiya.

Accessory lens elements are available for some cameras of this type that can be slipped on to change the focal length of both lenses. They convert the regular lenses to wide-angle or long focus, but are not an adequate solution to the problem of lens interchangeability.

The single-lens reflex is the best choice for use with long lenses (as when photographing wild animals) or for extreme close-ups (photographing wild flowers, for example). It will accept a wide range of lenses, although wide-angle lenses often pose problems with it because many of them extend far enough into the camera body to interfere with the movement of the mirror. There is another problem, too, with wide-angle lenses: their small images and great depth of field make it difficult to see when they are in sharp focus.

For some single-lens reflexes, manufacturers provide retrofocus wide-angle lenses. The retrofocus lens is like the 'true telephoto' (discussed in Chapter 3) in that it is asymmetrical. If the lens were taken out of the camera and turned around (as is often done in close-up work) the image would not focus at the same distance. In the 'true telephoto' the asymmetrical design is used to make the lens physically shorter than its optical focal length, to reduce the size and weight of the lens and camera combination; in the retrofocus the same principle is used to make the lens work farther from the film than its focal length in order to clear the mirror. Unfortunately, retrofocus lenses are hard to make and therefore expensive, and all but the best of them are plagued by internal reflections.

One signal advantage of the single-lens reflex is that it is the only camera design that can use variable focal length, or 'zoom' lenses. These lenses provide an infinite choice of focal lengths and the better ones remain in focus as the focal length is changed. There are already very many zoom lenses available and the range is likely to grow rapidly. Their main disadvantage is that they are not quite as fast as conventional lenses. The less expensive ones are also not as sharp.

It may be difficult with a single-lens reflex to judge focus accurately with lenses that are short, or slow, or both. A camera of this type that has a fully automatic diaphragm and mirror is much more convenient to use than one without these features.

The range-finder camera is usually lighter in weight, can be operated faster than any other type, and is the easiest to focus in dim light. Since the range finder is optically independent of the lens, it is equally accurate and equally bright for all lenses, fast or slow, long or short. Focusing is easy but seeing exactly what is included in the frame may be a bit difficult with other than normal lenses. Sometimes an accessory view finder is required, which means that the eye must be shifted from one window to another. The range finder cannot be used with very long lenses or for extreme close-ups, but the camera may be used with an accessory reflex viewing device, which, in effect, converts it into a single-lens reflex.

With these points firmly in mind, the photographer should be equipped to analyse his interests and make an enlightened choice based on his actual needs. He can thus prepare himself to face the camera salesman, who will doubtless persuade him to buy something entirely different from what he has chosen.

Small vs. Large

I have mentioned earlier my opinion that the size of the negative a camera uses is not, in itself, an important consideration in the choice of a camera. I realize that this is a controversial opinion.

The feud between the big-camera people and the small-camera people resembles nothing so much as the war between the Big-endians and the Little-endians in *Gulliver's Travels*. Otherwise rational people have spoken and written reams of emotion-laden nonsense attacking or defending a little assembly of glass and metal that has never bitten anyone. It appears that a small camera is like a snake in its ability to arouse the deepest and darkest anxieties of the human unconscious, though why this should be so is more obscure in the case of the camera.

Typically, the loudest voices are raised not in support but in condemnation of the small camera and those who use it. The '35-mm. man' is an irresponsible bohemian with no proper respect for craftsmanship and his elders. He takes dozens of pictures in order to get one good one. His pictures are grainy and lack 'quality'. Chances are he doesn't even have a sound grounding in technique.

If all this sounds reminiscent of the arguments about 'modern' art, that merely proves that photography is not so different from the other arts as we sometimes think. If there is an historical parallel, we can expect that small camera photography that seems avant-garde now will in time come to look old hat.

The big-camera man seems to a small-camera advocate to be a hidebound old fogey, blinded by prejudice to what is going on in the world. Listening to the big-camera man, it is hard to avoid the feeling that he opposes not only small negatives but also income tax, fluoridation of the water supply, and foreign aid, and favours corporal punishment for school children and tough treatment for drug addicts. In short, his watch goes 'tock-tick'.

Time seems to be on the side of the small-camera user. There are more of them and fewer of their opponents every year. Attitudes toward the small camera have shown a marked parallel to those toward the small automobile, changing in sequence from ridicule through scorn because it is 'cheap' to the idea that it is 'unsafe' and 'will not last' and on to eventual grudging acceptance and finally admiration.

Very little of this argument has any real basis in photography. Some of it, however, reflects simple misinformation. At the risk of getting caught in the cross fire, I am determined to present some facts that I think readers of this book have a right to expect.

Objectively, the negative or transparency is an intermediate step in the process of producing a finished picture—be it a print, projected image, or printed page. The size of the negative or transparency really has only a very minor and rather highly technical bearing on the end result. With a large camera more of the magnification is in the camera and less in the enlarger (with attendant depth-of-field problems, sometimes) but the total amount is the same.

Small cameras have certain definite advantages. Large cameras have others, but a large film size is not an advantage in itself.

The advantages claimed for the large film boil down to these:

1. 'Quality'   2. Detail
3. Lack of grain   4. Colour acceptable for publication

'Quality' is something produced by the person who does the work, not by the equipment with which he does it. Manufacturers would all like to have us believe that if we use their products our pictures will have 'quality', but of course there is no such guarantee. It may be easier for anyone to get the results he wants from equipment he has been using for years than from something new. This, however, is not an attribute of the equipment.

Detail, as shown in a picture, is dependent on many factors, of which film size is one of the least important. Those who find this hard to accept might consider the photography done for military reconnaissance.

It will not endanger anybody's national security to reveal that reconnaissance pictures are taken from altitudes of 40,000 feet and more, on 9 × 9-inch film. When asked how much could be learned from pictures taken from such a distance, a U.S. Defence Department spokesman answered, 'Well, we could tell if a household has a telephone, or a septic tank, and uses a rotary lawn mower.' Other experts mentioned that the pictures would show a golf ball on a fairway at a range of nine miles, and that the interpreters could read the unit designations painted on the bumpers of trucks. Reconnaissance satellites take pictures from an altitude of 150 miles, and objects the size of a car can be recognized from them.

In the face of such evidence, I am always startled when someone asks me (as they still do occasionally) whether 35-mm. negatives (which are roughly 1 × 1.5 inches) can be enlarged to 8 × 10. I am tempted to answer, 'Certainly. You mean eight by ten *feet*, of course.' In an exhibition of mine at The American Museum of Natural History there were several prints six feet wide, and they were made from badly over-exposed negatives made on old-fashioned thick emulsion 35-mm. film far inferior to what is available today.

Motion pictures are made with negatives only half the size of a 35-mm. still negative (because the longer dimension of the motion picture frame extends across the film instead of along it) and yet no one asks whether they can be enlarged to fill a screen forty feet wide. It is done every night.

Actually, the size of an enlargement is quite meaningless because we automatically hold a small print closer and a large one farther away. A mural-sized print viewed from across the room shows exactly the same definition as a postcard-size print of the same picture held in the hand. It is only when a small *portion* of the negative is enlarged that the degree of enlargement becomes important. Otherwise, the care used in exposure and processing is much more significant.

Grain is a much misunderstood and misused concept. It is cited as a disadvantage of small film as though there were some reason why pictures should not have grain. Silver grains are the building blocks of the photographic image. They belong in a photograph just as the weave of the canvas belongs in a painting. Etchings, lithographs, and engravings all have characteristic textures—so do photographs. The argument that there should be no grain in the picture because it is 'unnatural' rests on a misunderstanding of the distinction between the picture and the subject. A picture is not a duplicate of the subject; it is a new object made by means of silver grains. The presence of these grains is as natural in a photograph as the absence of them is to the subject. Adding grain represents less of a change from the original than translating the colours into tones of grey.

The valid question is whether the photographer has used the grain effectively. The size of the grain is one of the factors he controls. It is analogous to the type of brush stroke used in a painting; it may be harsh and crude or delicate and subtle. It cannot, however, be totally absent. In much current fashion photography, grain is emphasized, and sometimes added artificially for its graphic effect.

If a photographer is unable to control the grain in his pictures, the cause should be sought first in his technique, then in his equipment. Over-exposure, flare (internal reflections in the lens), and halation (internal reflections in the film) all cause an appearance of grain. Much of what is called grain is actually slight reticulation—the pebbly pattern produced by swelling and contraction of the gelatine that carries the emulsion. It is caused by changes in temperature during processing. The temperature and humidity at which the film is stored before processing and the speed with which it is dried afterward also affect the appearance of grain.

The final advantage claimed for large film is that it produces transparencies that are acceptable for publication. There is some historical basis for this belief, but it is long outdated. It is true that there was, at one time, a prejudice on the part of many editors against small transparencies. Longer ago there was a similar feeling about the size of the negatives from which black-and-white prints were made, but like all prejudices it faded when it was no longer possible to tell the ins from the outs.

The feeling against small colour transparencies lingered longer because using them once carried an economic penalty. The engraving cameras in common use prior to World War II had a maximum enlargement of about eight diameters. When small originals were enlarged more than eight times, the enlargement was done in two steps and more work was required, so the engravers charged a premium. When more modern equipment became available the engravers were understandably reluctant to abandon the premium charge, but eventually competition forced them to do so.

The use of small transparencies for reproduction was pioneered in the U.S.A. by the *National Geographic* magazine. In the 1940s, while some magazines were insisting that their photographers use 4 × 5-inch colour, the *Geographic* insisted that theirs use 35-mm. Kodachrome in Leicas.

Today, photographers for other magazines are frequently urged by their editors to use 35-mm. colour (though few editors today have the self-assurance to tell a photographer what camera to use). Among U.S. magazines that regularly use 35-mm. colour are *Life*, *Look*, and the *Saturday Evening Post* (with their large page size), *Show* and *Holiday* (with their excellent reproduction), *Fortune*, *Scientific American*, *National Geographic*, and *Natural History*. It is not unusual for a cover or full page to be reproduced from only a portion of a 35-mm. original.

The size of transparencies will soon be irrelevant, because

more and more work is being done on colour negatives, from which any size transparency or colour print can be made. Existing transparencies can be used to make negatives on a special inter-negative film. In some cases the printing plates are made directly from the negative, rather than from a positive. For the photographer who has difficulty selling small transparencies, using colour negative material would be a more forward-looking solution than using a larger camera.

To sum up: the large camera and the small camera each have distinct advantages for certain types of work, but there is no inherent advantage in a large film size. If a photographer is un-able to get satisfactory quality from any particular film size, the deficiency is in his technique rather than in the film, because other photographers do not encounter the same difficulty. One type or size of equipment may be more congenial to one individual than another type. Certainly, if a photographer is thoroughly familiar with his equipment and satisfied with the results, that is in itself an advantage of that equipment. If it will do what the photographer wants it to do, there is no reason to change it.

3:

Lens and Focus

PHOTOGRAPHS are possible because the light rays reflected by the subject are concentrated and 'resolved' by the lens into an image that is a miniature, reversed copy of the original. For every subject visible in front of the lens there is a corresponding image behind the lens—upside down and backward. It is also reversed in a third dimension—an object close to the front of the lens will project its image farther behind the lens, while the image of a faraway object will be resolved closer to the lens.

As long as the lens is open, a miniature world of images is suspended in space behind it. What we do when we 'focus' a camera is simply to decide which of these images will be intercepted by the film at the point where they are resolved or 'sharp'.

This can be demonstrated by taking the lens from a camera (or using a magnifying glass) and propping it on a table so that it points toward a window. The shutter and diaphragm should be open. Put a white card in the position usually occupied by the film, and you can see on the card the images projected by the lens. (It may be necessary to shade the card from any light not coming through the lens so that the projected images will not be washed out.)

If you start with the card well behind the normal film position and move it slowly toward the lens, the images of nearby objects will appear first, followed by those of things farther away. The images of distant objects—the view outside the window, for example—appear last, as the card is brought closer to the lens. Finally a point is reached at which the images disappear completely.

The point where the images of the most distant objects are resolved is called infinity, and the distance from that point to the centre of the lens is the focal length of the lens.

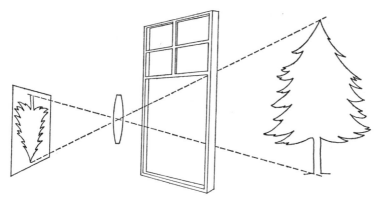

Fig. 4 Finding the images formed by a lens. A white card can be used to intercept the images behind a lens. The distance from the lens to the point where the images of the most distant objects appear is the focal length of the lens.

Focal Length and Viewpoint

Focal length is a built-in characteristic determined by the lens design. It controls the relationship between subject size and image size, subject distance and image distance. Other lens characteristics such as 'speed' (light-gathering power) and angle of view must be designed into the lens in relation to its focal length.

The focal length of a lens has a considerable effect on the appearance of the pictures made with it. A 'short' lens (one of short focal length) can be used close to the subject and will resolve the image a short distance behind the lens. With a 'long' lens, both distances will be proportionally increased to produce an image of the same size. But even though the images produced by the two lenses are the same size, they may not look the same. The difference in lens-to-subject distance produces differences in perspective, and it is these differences that are often called 'wide-angle effects' or 'telephoto effects'.

These 'effects' actually have nothing to do with the lens; they would be the same if the picture were made with a pinhole. They are results of the *viewpoint* from which the picture is taken.

If we stand squarely in front of a poster and look at the centre of it, the centre will actually be a little closer to us than the edges. If we photograph it from this spot, the centre will be rendered slightly larger, in proportion, than the edges. This will be true regardless of what lens we use. If we back away, so that the entire poster is farther away, the difference between the lens-to-centre distance and the lens-to-edge distance will be rapidly reduced as both distances increase, and the discrepancy will soon be too small to notice, although it is still theoretically present. In order to produce

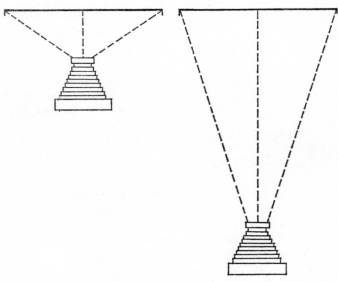

Fig. 5 *Viewpoint produces 'distortion'. Close up, the lens-to-centre distance is much shorter than the lens-to-edge distance and this produces 'distortion'. Farther away, there is less difference between lens-to-centre and lens-to-edge distances and therefore less 'distortion'.*

the same size image from our new, more distant viewpoint, however, we must use a longer lens. Hence the myth that long lenses reduce 'distortion'.

Actually, this kind of 'distortion' is perfectly normal and correct. Its proper name is foreshortening and it becomes more noticeable when we photograph a subject that is three dimensional (as most subjects are) rather than flat like the poster of our example. Foreshortening means simply that objects close to the camera (or the eye) are reproduced larger than those that are far away.

It is one of the cues that help people (and probably animals) to judge distances. The degree of foreshortening depends on the distance from viewpoint to subject.

Let us take the example of a beaver in front of his lodge (Fig. 6). If we photograph him from nearby, the beaver will be large and the lodge will be small because it is farther away from us. If we make the picture from a greater distance, the beaver and the lodge will both be smaller, but the *difference* between them will be reduced. The beaver-to-lodge distance is constant, but as the camera is moved back the lens-to-beaver distance and the lens-to-lodge distance both increase. The difference between them becomes smaller in proportion to the whole and so there is not as much difference in the magnification of their respective images. We can make the beaver appear the same size as he did in our close-up if we either change to a longer lens or enlarge a small portion of the negative, but in either case the lodge will be larger than it was in the nearby view. The effect is produced entirely by the distance from which the picture was taken, and not by the lens or camera.

The images formed in the eye are foreshortened just as much as the images formed in a camera, but the mind tends to compensate for differences in image size in accordance with what we 'know' the true size to be. Thus we do not think that a person who is close to us has a larger nose, in proportion to the size of his face, than one farther away. In a photograph, however, the difference may be noticeable. Since large noses are not considered ornamental in our culture, the portrait photographer, who has to flatter his subject to make a living, will photograph a person from a greater distance than would the family snap-taker. The photo-journalist seeking an eye-stopping effect might take a picture of the same subject from a much closer distance to exaggerate the size of his nose. If we assume that all three photographers are using the same size of film and want the same size image, then the portraitist would use a 'long' lens, the snap-taker a 'normal' lens, and the journalist a 'short' or 'wide-angle' lens. It is the choice of viewpoint, however, that determines the optical effect, not the choice of lens. If they had no choice of lenses the three photographers could still get their different effects by shooting from the same three viewpoints and enlarging different amounts of their negatives.

Although we do not ordinarily notice foreshortening when we

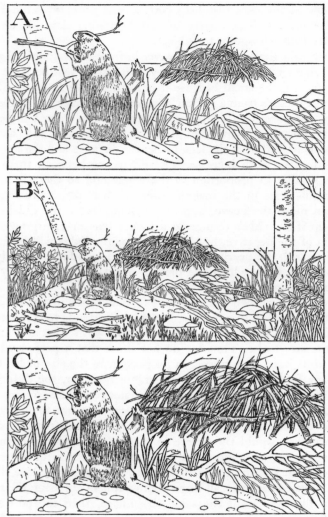

Fig. 6 *Viewpoint controls perspective.* A: *From nearby, the beaver (foreground) is large and his lodge (background) is small, being farther away.* B: *From a greater distance, there is less difference in size between the beaver and the lodge.* C: *In a picture taken from the same viewpoint as B, but with a longer lens, the beaver (foreground) can be shown the same size as in A, while the lodge (background) will be shown larger. The perspective in C is identical with the centre portion of view B.*

[1] *Mount Cook, New Zealand. A yellow filter preserves the sky tone and snow texture. Leaves at top 'frame' centre of interest, adding depth.* (*See page 91.*)

[2] *Wild horses on the moors of Newfoundland. 'Bad' weather sometimes improves a picture. (See page 17, dealing with grain.)*

[3] *Stream in Scotland. An example of depth of field. (See pages 30 to 36.)*

look at a scene, it is always present, and by long-standing habit it is associated in our minds with distance and depth. It has become part of our visual language, and can therefore be used in a photograph to influence 'mood' and create an illusion of a third dimension. The small camera, particularly when it is used with a very short lens, is said to produce photographs with a feeling of intimacy or immediacy, and it is often used for precisely that purpose in photo-journalism. These qualities are certainly visible, but they actually result from the foreshortening caused by the close distance at which the camera is used, rather than from the camera or lens itself. Conversely, the formal portrait needs a feeling of distance to 'put the subject on a pedestal' and remove him a little way from reality. Therefore a greater lens-to-subject distance and a longer lens are customarily used for formal pictures.

It may be useful to remember the following rules:

All lenses show the same perspective from the same viewpoint.

Lens-to-subject distance is proportional to focal length if image size is constant.

Image size is proportional to focal length if lens-to-subject distance is constant.

Although perspective is not a 'distortion' caused by the lens, there are, of course, some genuine sorts of distortion that poor lenses produce. There are even some that are caused by shutters. With modern, good-quality equipment they are rarely observed. Readers who need more information about them can find it in some of the reference works listed in the Bibliography.

The Normal Lens

A 'normal' lens is usually described as one that takes in a 'normal' angle of view—i.e., an angle similar to that of the eye. In reality the view seen by a human observer is much too complicated to be compared with a camera image. The mind uses a visual memory system to combine a series of images recorded as the eye darts over the scene, changing focus as it moves. The visual image really resembles a radar screen, where the glow lingers after the sweep has passed on, more than it resembles the static, delimited image made with a camera.

A lens taking in an angle of about 53° will produce pictures in which the perspective looks 'right' when the picture is viewed at a comfortable distance. What distance is comfortable depends, of course, on the size of the picture. Actually, there is only one distance from which the perspective in a picture will look exactly the same as it did in the original scene. If the entire negative is used to make the print, that distance will be equal to the focal length of the lens used to take the picture multiplied by the degree of enlargement (if any) of the print. For the full effect, the print must be viewed with only one eye.

Fortunately, ordinary picture-viewing does not require this degree of precision; pictures seen from an 'incorrect' distance will not look noticeably odd unless the disproportion is extreme, and even if it is it may serve a useful communicative purpose. But for ordinary, unspecialized photography embracing a wide range of subjects, the 'normal' lens gives a high proportion of pleasing pictures. It is also convenient to use under average shooting conditions.

Since the 'normal' lens is defined in terms of the angle it takes in (about 53°), it follows that a large film will need a larger image than a small film to include the same angle. Image size, as we have seen, is proportional to the focal length of the lens forming the image. Therefore, a normal lens for a large film will be longer than a normal lens for a small film. To take in the normal 53° angle, the focal length required works out to be roughly equal to the diagonal of the negative area. This can, of course, be measured, but it is more sporting to compute it by the Pythagorean theorem: the diagonal of a rectangle is the square root of the sum of the squares of the two dimensions. Any schoolboy (and an occasional adult) can thus readily determine that the normal lens for a 4 × 5-inch camera should be $6\frac{7}{16}$ inches in focal length (164 mm.), while a normal lens for a 35-mm. camera (which usually has a negative 24 × 36 mm. in size) would be just under 43 mm. in focal length.

In actual practice, 4 × 5-inch cameras have normal lenses of about 6-inch focal length and 35-mm. cameras use 50- or 55-mm. lenses as normal. There are several reasons for the discrepancy, but the main one seems to be that users of small films are more likely to use the entire negative area when making their prints.

The idea of the 'normal' lens is, of course, merely a convention, and there is nothing abnormal about using some other lens. The convention is not even consistent; portrait photographers normally use lenses that are longer than the diagonal of the film, while press photographers (who frequently have to work in cramped spaces) use, as 'normal', a lens shorter than the film diagonal.

Since all normal lenses take in the same angle, and since perspective is determined only by viewpoint, it follows that:

Any size camera will take the same picture from a given spot if its normal lens is used.

There are considerable differences in convenience between cameras of different sizes and types. The photographer will tend to take pictures in ways that are convenient with his particular camera, and it is this, rather than any optical difference, that gives the characteristic 'look' to pictures made with different kinds of cameras.

Lens Speed

The quantity of light that a lens can gather and project on to the film depends, as you might expect, on how big the lens is. A lens of longer focal length will produce a larger image but the lens must be correspondingly larger in diameter to produce the same brightness.

In other words, the 'speed' of a lens—the measure of the brightest image it can produce—is determined by its diameter in relation to its focal length. This is expressed in a ratio called an 'f number', because the letter 'f' is used to stand for the focal length in a sort of shorthand fraction. An $f/1$ lens is one whose maximum opening is the same as its focal length (f divided by 1). An $f/2$ lens has a maximum opening one half of its focal length (f divided by 2), and so on. Since the f number is really the bottom part of a fraction, a large aperture is represented by a small number and vice versa. The maximum aperture and focal length of a lens are usually engraved on its mount. On European and Japanese lenses the values are usually given thus: '1:2.5 = 3.5 cm'. An English or American lens would probably be marked '35 mm. $f/2.5$'. Both designations mean the same thing—the lens has a focal length of 35 mm. and its maximum aperture is 1/2.5 of that distance, or 14 mm. (I should say 'effective maximum aperture' because modern lenses are so complex in design that these elementary rules are subject to some exceptions, but unless you are designing lenses, you can safely ignore them.)

This brings us to one of the few real differences between large cameras and small cameras.

A lens with a speed of $f/2$ is not at all unusual on a 35-mm. camera. If it is the camera's normal lens, it will have a focal length of about 50 mm. and its inside diameter will be 50/2 or 25 mm.— about 1 inch. But a normal lens for a 4 × 5-inch camera, having a focal length of 6 inches, would have to have an inside diameter of 3 inches to achieve the same speed. A lens of such size would be so difficult to make that most users could not afford to buy one.

For such practical reasons, fast lenses are available only for small cameras, and this fact may dictate the choice of the small camera for work under inadequate light or with fast-moving subjects. The notion that fast lenses are 'better' than slow ones is very popular these days, but it is simply not true. Lens quality is related inversely, if at all, to lens speed.

Angle of View

All lenses of one focal length will produce the same image size at the same distance—image size meaning the size of the image of an object in front of the lens. Some such lenses, however, will include more of the scene than others. They have a wider angle of view. Since the image is on the same scale and more of it is included, it follows that a lens with a wide angle of view will 'cover' a larger-size film than a normal lens of the same focal length.

Normal lenses, as we have seen, are designed to take in an angle of about 53° in that part of their field that is projected on to the film. There is a little more around the edges that is not used unless the camera has adjustments that permit some alteration of the optical axis to solve special problems. (These movements, called swings and tilts, are discussed as attributes of the view camera in the preceding chapter.) A lens that takes in substantially more than a normal angle is called a wide-field or wide-angle lens. One that takes in less is called a long-focus or telephoto lens. (The name 'telephoto' correctly refers only to long-focus lenses of one special design, in which the physical length of the lens is shorter than its optical focal length to make it easier to handle, but it is so frequently misapplied to other long-focus lenses that the two terms are becoming synonymous.)

Like focal length and speed, angle of view is determined by the design of the lens. Angle of view refers to how much of the scene is included in the picture; it is not the same as covering power, which is the measure of the largest-size film that a lens can cover with a sharp, uniformly illuminated image, although, obviously, the two characteristics are related.

Focal length does not indicate the covering power of a lens. It may indicate the angle of view, but only in relation to a particular film size. A 100-mm. lens for a 35-mm. camera is a long-focus lens; a 100-mm. lens for a $2\frac{1}{4} \times 3\frac{1}{4}$-inch camera is a normal lens; a 100-mm. lens for a 4×5-inch camera is a wide-angle. The lens-to-film distance and image size are the same with all of them. The size of the entire field, however, varies with the covering power.

A lens will cover without difficulty any film *smaller* than that for which it was designed. Its covering power may be insufficient for a larger size, no matter what its focal length. The covering power of a lens is increased, however, when it is used for extreme close-ups, because as the lens-to-subject distance is reduced, the lens-to-film distance increases and the field grows proportionately. Extremely short lenses are often used to obtain great magnification in close-ups.

TABLE I

Some common sizes of lenses for 35-mm. cameras and their angles of view

Focal length	Angle	Focal length	Angle
21 mm.	92°	180	13.5
25	80.5	200	12
28	74	250	10
35	63	300	8
50	46	350	7
85	28.5	500	5
105	23.5	1000	2.5
135	18		

Table 1 gives the angles of view for lens sizes commonly used with 35-mm. cameras. The covering power is the same for all of them.

Depth of Field

An object in front of the lens is represented by an image behind the lens, the location and size of which depend upon the focal length, and the brightness upon the speed or aperture of the lens. There is another related variable: the depth of field, which also depends on these lens characteristics.

The object is 'in focus' when the camera is so adjusted that the film intercepts its image at the point where it is resolved or 'sharp'. Other objects nearer or farther than the one focused on will also be visible on the film, but their images will be unsharp, or 'out of focus'.

Objects close to the distance at which the camera is focused may, however, show no noticeable unsharpness. This is true because there is a zone around the point of focus that is close enough to being in focus to be indistinguishable from it. The size of that zone is the depth of field. (The size of the corresponding sharp zone at the film is called depth of focus, but the two terms are sometimes confused with one another.)

At normal distances the zone of sharpness extends about twice as far behind the point on which the lens is focused as it does in front of that point, and the farther away the focal point is, the deeper is the zone of sharpness. A handy way to visualize this is to draw two lines in pencil across a heavy rubber band. Then make a mark one third of the distance between them. Hold one end and move the other away from you. As you stretch the band you will see how the zone of sharp focus (the region between the two lines) grows as the focal point (the mark) moves farther away (see Fig. 7).

Depth of field also changes with lens aperture. Light rays from the subject that pass through the outer edges of the lens approach the film at a wider angle than those passing through the centre of the lens. Consequently the image they form spreads more rapidly before and behind the place where it is resolved. If the subject is not at the exact distance at which the camera is focused, its image is not intercepted by the film at its sharpest point, but slightly in front of or behind that point. The spreading of the light rays, and consequent unsharpness, will be reduced if we limit the light to that passing through the centre of the lens (see Fig. 8). This process, which reduces the lens aperture and therefore the amount of light reaching the film, is called 'stopping down'.

Stopping down is done with a variable diaphragm or iris,

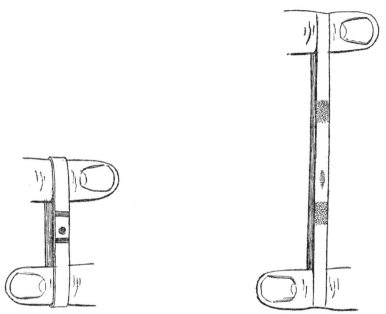

Fig. 7 How depth of field increases with distance. The zone of sharp focus grows as the focal point moves farther away. Sharp zone always extends about twice as far behind the point of focus as in front of it.

any given opening of which is called an '*f* stop'. The size of the opening is expressed as a proportion of the focal length, in the same manner as the maximum opening, or speed, of a lens. Aperture settings are usually marked with such numbers as 2, 2.8, 4, 5.6, 8, 11, 16, 22, 32, although there is no magic about the settings that happen to be marked. Intermediate ones can be used just as well.

The larger numbers, as will be remembered, represent smaller openings. The particular series of numbers given above is convenient because each opening admits one half as much light as the preceding one (the numbers are related by a factor of $\sqrt{2}$). A change from one of these apertures to the next is called 'one stop'. (An $f/2$ lens is one stop faster than an $f/2.8$ lens.) It may make the series easier to remember if we note that each number is approximately *twice* the number two places before it in the series.

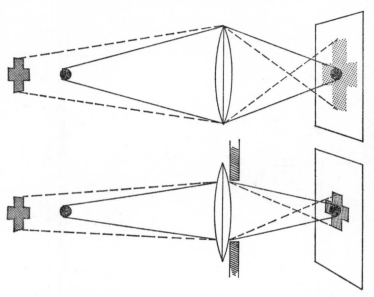

Fig. 8 *Why depth of field increases as the lens is stopped down.* Above: *The wide-open lens is focused on the dot and the dot's image on the film is sharp. The light rays from the cross, which is beyond the focal point, are focused in front of the film and spread out rapidly owing to the wide angle at which they meet.* Below: *The lens is still focused on the dot, but the aperture has been decreased. The light rays from the cross still meet in front of the film, but because they meet at a smaller angle, they also spread out less rapidly, producing a smaller and therefore sharper image on the film.*

Depth of field depends upon focal length, aperture, and the distance at which the lens is focused. Tables showing depth of field at various distances and apertures are published for every lens, and depth-of-field scales are engraved on the lens mount or around the focusing knob on most cameras. It is astonishing how few people know how to use them. Their use is explained in the next section, Using Depth of Field.

One of the advantages claimed for small cameras is that their short lenses 'have greater depth of field'. An examination of the depth-of-field tables for several interchangeable lenses will show that the shorter ones do, indeed, have greater depth of field at any given aperture. There is a catch, however. The shorter lenses also produce smaller images. If when we change lenses we also move closer to the subject so that the image size remains constant, the depth of field will be exactly the same! If we use a longer lens but move back, so that the image is still small, we will find the depth of field unchanged from that of the short lens. In other words:

All lenses have the same depth of field at any given aperture if image size is constant.

In practice, however, image size does not need to be constant and on this fact depends one of the real advantages of small cameras and short lenses. The image size we are concerned with is that on the negative. But the negative is only an intermediate step in the making of the finished product—a print, projected image, or printed page. It really does not matter whether the negative is large or small, so long as it produces the same end result. In the camera, a three-dimensional subject is translated into a two-dimensional image, and it may be difficult to get sufficient depth of field within the limitations of the light available and the shutter speed required. In the next stage of the process— translation of the two-dimensional negative image into a two- dimensional print—depth of field is no problem. It is often useful to work with a small image on the negative and do the enlarging in the darkroom instead of in the camera.

It is not the short lens but the *small image* that has greater depth of field. Exactly the same result can be obtained by using a long lens at a greater distance. A small negative image does not have to be on a small film, either; it can be on a portion of a large film. The only difference is one of convenience. The small camera is convenient, too, in some other respects, and it is that convenience, rather than any optical superiority, that explains its popularity.

P.N.   D

Using Depth of Field

Many people believe that the right way to focus a camera is to focus on the subject and then stop down the lens to make the image sharper. This procedure conceals two assumptions, neither of which is always correct. Unless the object you are photographing is flat and faces the camera squarely (like a poster), it may be best not to focus on it. Rather, you should locate the nearest and farthest objects that should be sharp (the closest and most distant people in a picnic group, for example), and then select a point of focus and a lens opening which will include both extremes in the zone of sharp focus. This is easiest to do with a camera that has a range finder. Optical range finders were originally developed not for focusing cameras but for measuring distances, and they will still do so. Simply focus on the farthest object and note the distance to it as shown on the scale; then focus on the nearest object and note *that* distance. Then set the camera so that the same aperture marking is opposite each of these distances on the depth-of-field scale. This aperture is the maximum opening that will bring them both into focus, and is usually the one to use. The shutter speed required for the film you are using and the amount of light you have can be read opposite this aperture on a light meter. Of course, if the speed you get by this method is impracticable, you may have to use another aperture, change film, or eliminate something from the picture.

Stopping down farther will not make the image any sharper. To be sure, it will make the zone of sharp focus deeper, but this is not always useful. Furthermore, it *may* make the image less sharp, especially with a fast lens. Fast lenses are admirably designed to do a good job at maximum aperture, but they pay for this by beginning to lose sharpness when stopped down beyond a certain point. This point varies from lens to lens but is usually around two thirds of maximum opening. Slow lenses (those with smaller maximum openings, represented by larger *f* numbers) are likely to be sharper than fast lenses when stopped down.

Zone focusing, as described above, can be used to advantage even on subjects that won't stand still long enough for you to read off the nearest and farthest distances. If, for example, you are going to photograph the finish of a horse race, you can set your camera to include in the zone of sharp focus everything on the finish line from the near rail to the far one. You'll be reasonably sure of getting the winner in this zone.

The folly of unnecessary stopping down is particularly obvious when everything in the picture is far away, as is the case in pictures taken from the air or photographs of distant landscapes. After all, it does no good to have a deep zone of focus if there's nothing in the zone. Similarly, there is no point in stopping down when the zone of focus already extends to infinity. It's true that stopping down will bring the foreground into focus, but for every foot of depth gained in front of the focal point, the sharp zone will also include two feet behind it—wasted when everything behind the subject is already in focus.

Hyperfocal Distance

In our experiment with the rubber band we saw that the zone of focus became deeper as it moved away from us. When the far limit of the sharp zone reaches infinity, the zone reaches its maximum depth. The camera is still not focused at infinity; it is focused at a distance that will cause the sharp zone to extend to infinity. Since the extent of the sharp zone depends on the aperture, this distance will also depend on the aperture. It is called the hyperfocal distance for that particular lens length and opening.

Focusing on a point farther away than the hyperfocal distance for the lens/aperture combination you are using is useless. It will *reduce* the depth of the sharp zone, because the near edge of the zone will recede while the far edge will remain at infinity since it cannot be any farther away.

Hyperfocal distance should be used whenever sharpness is desired all the way back to infinity. It is also the place to set the focus for scenes in which everything is a considerable distance from the camera, and for situations where it may be necessary to shoot quickly without focusing. The hyperfocal distance for any lens and aperture may be found in the depth-of-field table or on the depth-of-field scale on the camera or lens. It is not necessary to read it; the camera can be focused at hyperfocal distance simply by placing the infinity mark on the scale opposite the lens opening being used. The near limit of the sharp zone can be read from the scale opposite the same lens opening on the other side of the scale (Fig. 9).

If you need more depth to get everything in, use a smaller aperture; if you don't need so much, open up. But in either case you should refocus as you change aperture so that the aperture you are using still falls opposite infinity on the scale. Of course, you must also compensate for the change in lens opening by a corresponding change in shutter speed.

The use of zone focusing and hyperfocal distance (which is simply a zone that ends at infinity) will often permit you to use

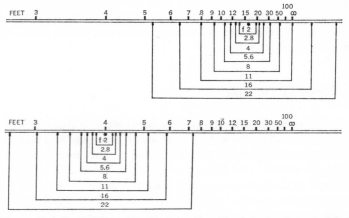

Fig. 9 Depth-of-field scale for 50 mm., f/2 lens is shown with lens focused at 17 feet, top, hyperfocal distance for f/11. At 4 feet, below, sharp zone is reduced. Depth-of-field scales are engraved on lens mount or focusing knob of most cameras.

higher shutter speeds or slower film, and thereby produce a sharper image. But it is by no means necessary or desirable to have everything in a picture sharp. The eye does not see everything as sharp: differences in sharpness help us to perceive depth, in a photograph as in real life. (This is one reason why old-style advertising photographs, which were uniformly sharp throughout, looked so phony.) There is no basis for the belief that a sharp image is inherently 'better' than an unsharp one. Each has its own power to convey information or set a mood. Focus is part of the language of photography. The reason for learning how it works is to be able to use it—like any other technique—to make your pictures say what you want them to say.

4:

Film and Exposure

AFTER an image is formed in the camera, as discussed in the preceding chapter, it is translated into a corresponding, but by no means identical, image on film.

'Exposure' is the most convenient name for this process. It involves much more than simply deciding how to set the controls on the camera. Properly used, exposure is one of the tools the photographer has at hand to make the picture say what he wants it to say. We have only to think of terms like sombre, grey, dull, and shadowy or bright, sunny, sparkling, and luminous to realize the emotional connotations of light. In photographs, the rendering of light is controlled by exposure.

This is not to say that a dull, dark scene can be made to look scintillating by proper choice of exposure. There are limits. But the appearance of light in photographs, and with it the mood, is subject to more control through exposure than most photographers realize. There is no such thing as *the* correct exposure for a picture. There may be many different exposures which will yield an acceptable print without too much manipulation during printing. The choice of one or another is part of the creative process and not a technical matter at all. But the photographer must understand the technical process in order to use it creatively.

When light strikes a film it causes a chemical change in the emulsion that produces a deposit of silver grains when the film is developed. The concentration of these grains is roughly proportional to the amount of light that struck the film. This amount of light can be an intense light for a short time or a weaker light for a longer time. Within limits, either combination will produce the same concentration of silver grains, or density. We can control the amount of light reaching the film by opening or closing the diaphragm (or iris) on the lens, and/or by controlling the length of time the shutter is open. This is easy to visualize if we use the analogy of a glass of water. Obviously, we can fill a glass to a certain level by pouring water through a large hole for a short time or through a small hole for a longer time.

Changing the size of the lens opening has other results, as we have seen in Chapter 3. It affects the depth of field. Changing the length of time the shutter is open (shutter speed) also has other results in addition to controlling the exposure. It changes the degree to which motion will be 'stopped'; not only the motion of the subject, if there is any, but also the motion of the camera itself. Determining what combination of lens opening and shutter speed to use therefore involves four factors: the amount of light available, the speed of the film, the depth of field needed, and the shutter speed required to stop motion (if that is desired).

Reconciling these four factors often requires a compromise. Fortunately, modern films (except those designed for special purposes) have considerable 'latitude'. That is, they will produce acceptable images from a fairly wide range of exposures. These images are not, however, identical. The image produced by a generous exposure does not look the same as the image produced by a scant exposure, even though both may be printable. The reason for this is that the response of films to light is not 'linear'. There is no direct and uniform relation between the amount of light falling at one point on the film and the resulting density of silver. The relation is fairly uniform within certain limits, but beyond those limits the film cannot follow. The mathematical way of expressing this is as a response curve (see Fig. 10) that has a straight portion in the middle and a curve at each end. The upper curve is called the shoulder, the lower curve is called the toe. Only exposures falling on the straight part of the response curve will be reproduced accurately. This is not necessarily a disadvantage, because the finished product—a photographic print, transparency, or a printed page—usually is capable of much less range from light to dark than the original scene. The lightest tone possible in a photographic print, for example, is the white of the unexposed paper; the darkest is the black produced by full exposure in printing. All the tones of the original subject must in some manner be compressed into the range of the final print. The useful range of the film is usually less than the brightness range of the subject, but greater than the range of the paper print. Thus, there is a two-stage compression of the tonal range—from scene to negative and again from negative to print. The extent of this compression, and also the region (highlight or shadow) where most of the 'squeezing' occurs, can be controlled by proper selection of exposure and development.

The human eye and mind can accept an enormous range of light intensities—far more than any film can record. The photo-

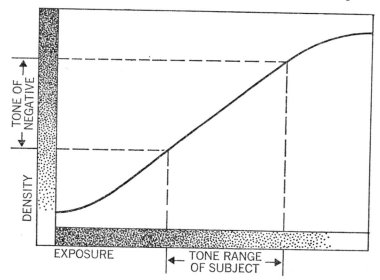

Fig. 10 *A typical response curve showing the relation of exposure to density on the negative. Exposure determines where the tones of subjects will fall on the curve (the greater the exposure, the farther to the right on the curve). Only values falling on the straight portion of the curve will be reproduced in their proper relationship. Above and below the straight portion, tones will not be adequately differentiated, making dark colours appear black and light ones appear white.*

grapher must allow for this fact in selecting his exposure. He must recognize, for example, that if he photographs a scene in which the sun sparkles on the surface of a stream running through a dark forest, no film can preserve as much detail in both the bright reflections and the dark shadows as the eye can see in the original scene. The photographer must choose to emphasize one or the other, or sacrifice some of each.

Occasionally it happens that a subject has a shorter range of tones than is needed to produce a normal print. In that case, exposure and development are altered to expand, instead of compress, the tone range.

Light Meters

Old-time photographers used to pride themselves on their ability to guess correct exposures. They generally worked under fairly uniform conditions, however, and used only one or two kinds of film. A light meter is absolutely indispensable for the wide range of materials and picture-taking conditions encountered today. But the old-timers' judgment is not obsolete; it is still needed to interpret the meter's readings.

There are a few 'spot' meters that are capable of measuring the brightness of small areas in a scene, but they are comparatively bulky, expensive, and temperamental. Most light meters used for ordinary picture-taking are of the 'integrating' type, which means that they measure the average intensity of light over whatever area they cover.

Obviously, an average reading is apt to be wrong if the subject is very different in brightness from its surroundings. A skier seen against a snow-covered hillside or a sunlit wild flower in a dark forest will not be properly exposed if an average reading is used. It may be difficult or impossible in cases like these to measure the brightness of the subject itself.

Similarly, although it is less obvious to the eye, the sky is often many times brighter than anything on the ground, particularly on an overcast day. Most reflected light meters should be pointed slightly downward whenever the sky is included in their view, to reduce the proportion of sky light reaching the meter.

Where the range of brightness is great, readings must be taken so as to measure the brightness of the subject and not the background. In fact, a photographer would not go far wrong if he adopted, as a rule of thumb, the practice of basing exposure solely on the brightness of the subject and ignoring the surroundings. In some cases, however, the range of the film would be insufficient to accommodate both.

Another approach is to measure not the light reflected by the subject but the light falling on it. This method assumes that where the subject is dark it is to be rendered dark and where it is light it should be rendered light. Exposure is therefore based on a middle value between light and dark. In a brightness scale extending from zero reflectance to 100 per cent reflectance, the midpoint is not 50 per cent, as might be expected, because like most aspects of perception, the brightness scale is logarithmic. That is, brightness is perceived in steps that increase geometrically rather than arithmetically. Equal steps are 1, 2, 4, 8, 16, 32, not 1, 2, 3, 4, 5, 6. If it is measured in steps that appear equal to an observer, the point which is half the number of steps from full black to full white will be a grey that reflects about 18 per cent of the light falling on it. Theoretically, then, if we expose in such a way that this middle point is in the middle of our exposure range, the exposure should be correct. This is often done in studio photographs, where the range of the lighting and the brightnesses of the subject matter are under the photographer's control. A grey card of 18 per cent reflectance is held in front of the subject and the reading taken from it. Alternatively a white card can be used and the reading divided by five. ('White' card stock has a reflectance of about 90 per cent—5 × 18.)

A more primitive method of doing the same thing is to take a reading of your own hand. The hand of a photographer of Caucasian stock has a reflectance of about 36 per cent, so the reading obtained should be divided by two. The most convenient way to divide exposures is on the shutter-speed dial. To divide by 5, for example, use the diaphragm opening that falls opposite 1/10 sec. but use it at 1/50. To divide by 2, take the diaphragm opening given for 1/50 and use it with 1/100. Any other analogous combination will do as well.

Whenever a substitute is used to determine exposure instead of the actual subject, the following conditions must be met: the substitute object must be lighted to the same degree and preferably in the same way as the subject; the meter must be held far enough away from the object so that it does not read its own shadow; and at the same time it must be close enough so that it reads only the object and not any of the surroundings. This point can usually be identified by moving the meter up to the object until a point is reached where the reading 'levels off' and does not change as the meter moves. That point is usually the one at which the object fills the entire field of the meter.

A measurement of the light falling on the subject (instead of that reflected by it) is called an 'incident light' reading. There are a number of meters that measure incident light directly without a grey card, and some that have attachments to measure either incident or reflected light.

The incident light method gives no warning of brightnesses that may be beyond the range of the film, since it averages all the light falling on the grey card or meter cell, ignoring differences in illumination between different parts of the scene. It also ignores the lighting contrast—the ratio of light coming from one direction to that coming from other directions.

If a reflected-light meter is simply pointed at the scene from the camera position it averages all the light reflected from the area it covers. The better meters cover an angle (called the 'angle of acceptance') roughly equal to the coverage of a normal focal-length lens, but some meters cover a substantially wider angle and may, therefore, be misled by areas that are not in the picture. No meter can distinguish between the important parts of a picture and the unimportant ones. With average reflected light readings, a small dark subject against a light background will be under-exposed; a light subject against a dark background will be over-exposed.

Either the incident or reflected light method will give usable results in a large proportion of picture-taking situations. Neither is as accurate as reading the highest and lowest brightnesses and determining, for that particular picture, the best intermediate exposure. With anything other than a spot meter, the brightnesses of small areas can be read only at close range, an obvious impossibility in some situations. Sometimes it is equally impossible to measure the light falling on the subject because the subject is not accessible (a distant mountain, for example). In such cases, an over-all reading, interpreted in the light of experience, is the best guide.

Reflected light readings have a built-in bias in a generally useful direction: if the scene is dark in colour a reflected light reading will call for more exposure than an incident light reading. If the scene is light in colour the reflection meter will call for less exposure than the incident light meter, which will give the same reading in both cases if the illumination is the same.

Because it is useful to move a meter around so as to 'read' small areas and different parts of the scene, meters that are attached to the camera are not a good choice. They make it necessary to move the entire camera to take a reading of one area. In any case, the small size imposed on such meters does not make for high quality.

Meters using cadmium sulphide cells are much more sensitive than the older selenium-cell meters. This increased sensitivity is most welcome, because modern films are capable of taking pictures in light too dim to measure with a selenium-cell meter. CdS meters can be made sensitive enough to read the intensity of the image directly on the ground glass—a great advantage with inaccessible subjects or when photographs are taken through telescopes, microscopes, or other instruments.

The great sensitivity and small size of CdS cells, however, are offset by three outstanding disadvantages. First, they are not reliable at low temperatures. Second, they are sensitive to one colour of light and not to others. A cell sensitive to blue-green, for example, will give an incorrect reading in the late afternoon, when the light is predominantly reddish. Different types of cells respond to different colours of light, but none of them corresponds to the sensitivity of any commonly used film. Third, the cells adjust slowly to changes in the light. If a CdS meter is used outdoors and then taken inside where there is much less light, the reading will decline gradually instead of dropping at once to the proper level.

These limitations mean that a CdS meter is useful chiefly as a second meter, to be used only in dim light or special situations where the regular meter will not function.

The new cadmium selenide (CdSe) meters, combining the sensitivity of cadmium sulphide with the colour response of selenium, may well supersede both types within the next decade.

Tonal Range and Film Sensitivity

As we have seen, an exposure that is right for the main subject may place the background or some other part of the picture beyond the brightness range that the film can accommodate. The best way of dealing with this problem is by using filters, which are discussed in the next chapter. Sometimes, however, the subject itself has a range of tones so great or so small that the exposure must be altered to accommodate it. If the range is very great, the photographer may have to lose some separation in either the highlights or the shadows, i.e., in the photograph there will be less difference in tone between adjacent steps in the tone scale than there is in the subject. The extremes may fall above or below the range in which the film can record them without distortion—or, to put it in mathematical terms, above or below the straight-line portion of the curve.

Values lying on the straight portion will be compressed or expanded according to the slope or steepness of that line. Different films and different developers produce different amounts of slope, or contrast. So do differences in developing time. Increasing development time increases contrast and also increases the density of the image, bringing it closer to the maximum permitted by the film, when all the silver grains available are exposed. Then the tones will not be adequately separated, and highlights may show no detail at all. This effect is called 'blocking up' of the highlights.

It follows, therefore, that a subject with a short tonal range should have a scant exposure and generous development, while a subject with a great range of tones should have a generous exposure and scant development. This is expressed in another form in the old photographer's saying, 'Expose for the shadows and develop for the highlights', which dates, of course, from an era when all films were developed by inspection under a red safelight. It produces exactly the same result. The extent to which exposure and development can be varied will depend on the film and developer used. Characteristic curves for most common film and developer combinations are published in photographic handbooks.

With small sizes of film, where there are many exposures on a roll, it is seldom convenient to give different amounts of development to different frames. This is, in fact, one of the most persuasive arguments in favour of the larger camera that uses sheet film. But in any case the cost of film is a small item in the picture-taking budget, and it is worthwhile to use several rolls instead of one and develop them differently, as the subjects require. It is possible to rewind a partially used 35-mm. film and take it out of the camera, then later put it back and use the remainder. There is even one camera (the Exakta) that has a little knife inside it to cut off the used portion of the film so that the remainder can be exposed and developed differently. In this camera the film can be fed from one cassette (a re-usable film cartridge) to another so that the used portion will not be fogged when the camera is opened to remove it. A short piece of the unused film is exposed to the light. It is used to feed the film into a new take-up cassette, and thus becomes the 'leader' of a new, abbreviated roll.

It is possible to compute exposure so precisely that every spot in the scene will be represented by an exact, predetermined shade of grey in the final print. Ansel Adams, dean of American landscape photographers, is the author of a widely admired system for doing this. It is rather too time-consuming for photography of live subjects, however, and even with landscapes there would be a danger that the sun might set before the exposure computation was finished. Fortunately, such precision is seldom necessary.

At the beginning of this chapter it was stated that, within limits, the same exposure could be produced by a large lens-opening and a short exposure-time or by a small lens-opening and a long exposure-time. This interchangeability is called 'reciprocity'. When the limits are reached and the relation between speed and aperture is no longer constant, the result is described as 'reciprocity failure'. It is encountered occasionally in ordinary picture-taking.

Extreme Exposure Times

At very long and very short exposure times, films show less sensitivity than would be calculated from their performance at normal speeds. Exposure times short enough to show this effect cannot be achieved by most mechanical shutters, but they are encountered when electronic flash of very short duration is used. At the other end of the scale, reciprocity failure will be noted in some long time exposures. The effect is much more marked in colour than in black-and-white because of the complexity of colour film. The three emulsions of which colour film is composed have different speeds and are affected differently by reciprocity failure. Therefore, with colour film there are changes not only in exposure but also in the balance of the three colours. For this reason, the exposure indexes of colour films are calculated at a speed appropriate to the use for which they are intended, and in some types there are different films for long and for short exposures. The data sheets packed with the film give information on correcting both exposure and colour balance at a few sample exposure times.

These corrections are not to be ignored, because in some cases they require more than a ten-fold increase in exposure. In extreme close-ups a considerable increase in exposure is required to compensate for the magnification (see Chapter 8) and the combined effect of the two corrections is enough to make an accurately measured, but uncorrected, exposure produce a baffling sheet of blank film. If expressed in exposure factors, one correction must be multiplied by the other. If the reciprocity factor is 5 and the magnification factor is 4 (as it is for a same-size reproduction) the indicated exposure must be multiplied by 20!

It is often convenient to express exposure information in terms of stops, because they are logarithmic, like our perception of brightness differences. Differences that appear equal to us will be equal in terms of stops, not in terms of factors. A stop is a factor of 2. Since they are logarithms, they are added rather than multiplied. A reciprocity factor of $2\frac{1}{3}$ stops and a magnification factor of 2 stops equal a total correction of $4\frac{1}{3}$ stops. This is the same correction as that given above. The two scales can be compared on the computer dial of an exposure meter, where the shutter speeds are expressed in fractions of a second, and the apertures in f numbers, usually at intervals of one stop (1.4, 2, 2.8, 4, 5.6, 8, 11, 16, 22, etc.).

What Is Sharpness?

Films have several different characteristics that contribute to the appearance of sharpness in a picture. This appearance is, however, a subjective impression and is strongly influenced by non-photographic considerations. For example, a familiar object which can readily be recognized will generally appear sharper in a picture than an unfamiliar object, under identical conditions. The characteristics of the film that contribute to sharpness do not necessarily occur together in all cases. They are often lumped together in popular language under names like 'sharpness', 'definition', or 'resolution'. Their absence is often referred to as 'grain'. Actually these terms have precise technical meanings, but only an expert with laboratory equipment can distinguish among them.

It is widely believed that grain is the limiting factor in sharpness and that it is inversely proportional to film speed (i.e., fast films are grainy and slow films are not grainy). This is a drastic and mis-leading over-simplification. A great deal of what is believed to be grain in photographs is actually low-level reticulation caused by poor temperature control during processing. Over-exposure also causes graininess, and so does over-development or an out-of-focus image. The conditions under which film is stored, exposed, and processed all affect the sharpness of the negative and the appear-ance of grain. High humidity during storage and excessive im-mersion time in processing cause the emulsion to swell unevenly and produce a grainy effect. For maximum sharpness, films should receive minimal exposure and development and should be processed, washed, and dried in as short a time as possible.

Although suggestions on processing are not within the scope of this book, these facts are mentioned simply to point out that the appearance of sharpness is not controlled solely by the choice of film. In actual practice, photographers rarely use all the sharpness of which a film is capable.

There are at least three scientifically measurable attributes of film that contribute to the appearance of sharpness: graininess, resolving power, and acutance. They are closely related to the spreading of light within the emulsion. Modern films are sharper than old-fashioned ones because we have learned how to make emulsions thinner. But all these factors together are less important than the mental processes that occur when the picture is viewed. All things considered, the appearance of sharpness, like the appearance of 'true' colour, is largely in the eye of the beholder.

Light Sources

Most photographers who are interested in nature subjects have a corresponding fondness for natural light. Certainly it has great advantages. It is free and does not have to be transported; it provides an ever-changing panoply of lighting effects so varied that no photographer could think of them all; and it provides the appearance of 'roundness' and 'depth', so difficult to achieve with artificial light.

The reason why artificial light does not look like sunlight is this: light diminishes in intensity ('falls off' is the term photographers use) in proportion to the square of the distance from the light source. With artificial sources this means that objects close to the light receive a great deal more illumination than those farther away. The sun, however, is so far away from everything on the earth that the difference in distance between near and far objects is negligible. Daylight is 'rounded' because there is no great difference in the illumination from one plane to another and also because light is reflected from the sky on all sides to light up the shadows.

Despite these advantages, natural light alone cannot be used for every photograph. When artificial light must be used it should, so far as possible, be made to look like natural light. In no case should the lighting intrude or call attention to itself. Artificial light will usually look more natural if it is not aimed directly at the subject but reflected or 'bounced' off of a wall, ceiling, or large reflector. Floodlights, flash bulbs, and the few electronic flash bulbs that have removable reflectors will often give more natural-looking lighting indoors if used without reflectors so that part of the light is bounced from the walls and ceiling. Light can also be diffused with cloth, paper, or spun glass. Small objects can be surrounded with a 'tent' which will serve as a reflector if lighted from within or a diffuser if lighted from without.

Any method that diffuses the light reduces its intensity. If every bit of light is needed, the light should be softened by reflecting back into the shadow areas whatever light would otherwise fall outside the picture area. Diffusers and reflectors used for colour photography (including walls and ceilings used for bouncing) must be white or grey. Otherwise they will colour the light.

Floodlights have the obvious advantage that their effect on a stationary subject can be studied. Their chief disadvantage is the heat they produce, which is enough to rule them out for some fragile subjects.

Flash bulbs have come back into favour following the development of more compact types with considerable light output. Most of the ills associated with flash photography result from using a single flash bulb at the camera. Almost any deviation from that pattern will bring an improvement in the lighting; adding a large, flat reflector on the shadow side of the subject, using more than one light source, or even moving the flash away from the camera on an extension cord. The newer, small-sized flash bulbs make it more practical than ever to use more than one flash for a picture.

[4] *Adélie penguins congregate on ice floes. Polar skuas circle overhead. Taken with a zoom lens, as it was impossible to change the viewpoint. (See page 115.)*

[5] *Newfoundland fishermen.* (See page 3.)

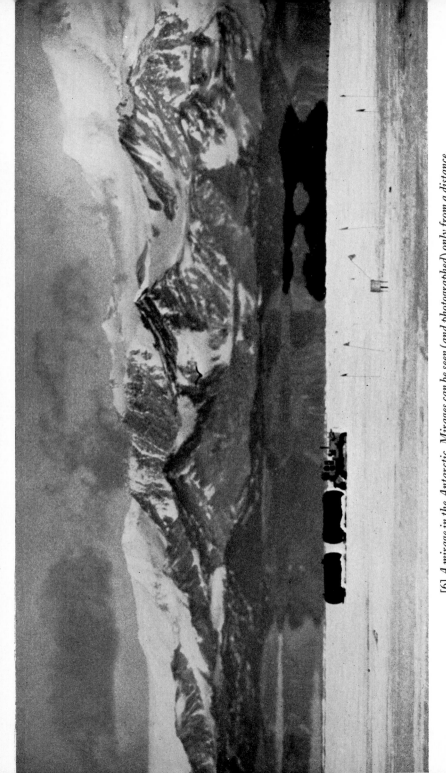

[6] *A mirage in the Antarctic. Mirages can be seen (and photographed) only from a distance. This one, about forty miles away, was photographed with a 600-mm. zoom lens.*

The extra flash units need not be connected to the camera; 'slave' units are triggered by the light from one bulb that is fired by the camera. One professional trick is to use the slave units as the main light sources and use only enough light at the camera to make them fire. This is accomplished by choosing a relatively weak bulb, aiming it away from the subject, or removing the reflector.

Electronic flash produces a softer effect than flash bulbs and is the only means of achieving exposures shorter than about 1/1000 sec. with ordinary cameras. Not all electronic flash units are fast, however. The large studio units that operate from power lines are usually fairly fast; the small, battery-powered portable units get more total light output by using a longer flash—in some cases as slow as 1/500 sec. Electronic flash units are easily rigged as slave units and will all fire at the same instant (with flash bulbs there is a small time lag between the triggering flash and the slave).

The chief disadvantage of flash—electronic or bulb—is that the photographer cannot see what he is getting. Various techniques have been devised to overcome this limitation. Some studio electronic flash units have small incandescent 'modelling lights' attached to or built into the flash heads to show approximately how the lighting will look. One can set up large reflectors with flood lamps in them to judge the effect, then take out the floods and substitute flash bulbs (after disconnecting the power), but all these methods are cumbersome and unreliable. A more precise method is to use a camera that will accept a Polaroid adaptor for making test exposures. With practice one can learn to judge exposure as well as lighting from such tests. Electronic flash is convenient where tests are to be made because it will repeat its performance indefinitely. Obviously, though, some subjects will not wait around for a second shot.

Another disadvantage of flash is the difficulty of determining a correct exposure. There are meters that will read the intensity of an instantaneous flash, but they are bulky and expensive. They are a special form of incident light meter, and do not reveal the lighting contrast (the range between highlight and shadow areas) or take into account the colour of the subject.

The usual method of computing flash exposures is with guide numbers. The method of deriving these numbers for flash bulbs has now been standardized so they are less unreliable than they used to be, but they still have to be corrected for many variables.

Guide numbers for electronic flash are computed differently by different manufacturers. The guide number for a particular combination of film, shutter speed, and flash bulb is equal to the lens opening that produces an optimum exposure multiplied by the bulb-to-subject distance in feet. The guide number is a constant because, as we mentioned, the light falls off according to the square of the distance from the source, and the lens openings are designated by a logarithmic series of numbers. Thus to find the correct lens opening it is only necessary to divide the guide number given by the manufacturer of the flash by the distance from flash to subject. A guide number of 100 at a distance of 10 feet gives $f/10$ as the lens opening.

In practice, exposures found by guide number must be modified to suit the conditions. Outdoors the exposure should be increased (by using a larger lens opening, designated by a smaller number) to compensate for the absence of reflected light, such as is found indoors. Light subjects require a little less exposure; dark subjects a little more. Guide numbers should always be checked by making a series of test exposures with any new camera, light, or reflector.

A single artificial light source is almost never satisfactory unless there is light from other directions to balance it. Reflectors of cardboard, cloth, or metal foil can be used to make one light source do the work of several. Alternatively, several sources can be used. The latter arrangement would be the best choice if, for example, nocturnal visitors are to be photographed at a water hole. Several flash units should be deployed so as to give reasonably rounded lighting. (See Chapter 12.)

In some situations, flash is used together with some other light source. It may be used to light up the shadows in a picture made with daylight, or it may light the foreground while something else —the sun or a night skyline—lights the background. The exposure is computed by finding the lens opening required for the flash, then determining the shutter speed that will give a satisfactory exposure for the fixed light at that lens opening.

For example: Suppose we are to photograph an aquarium in front of a window, the aquarium to be lighted with electronic flash in order to stop the motion of the fish. We set up the flash units, being careful to avoid reflections in the glass, and measure the distance from them to the centre of the tank. The distance is 4 feet and the guide number is 100, so the lens opening should be $f/25$ (the nearest marked stop is $f/22$, which is close enough). At that lens opening, however, the window would be under-exposed unless we used a slow shutter speed, so we take a meter reading for the window, set the computer on the meter, and read opposite $f/22$ the shutter speed 1/25 sec. This is the speed to use. The electronic flash will give all of its light within 1/1000 sec. in any case, so increasing the exposure time will have no effect on it. The extra time will record the window.

In this example it would be necessary to prevent window light from reaching the aquarium (by placing a sheet of cardboard behind it, perhaps) so that the moving fish would not appear as blurred or ghost images during the long exposure intended to record the window.

When flash is used to 'fill in' shadows in pictures made with daylight, the flash must be subdued so that it does not overpower the daylight or present an unnatural appearance. Therefore, less exposure (a smaller lens opening, designated by a higher number) is used in such a case than would be used if the flash were the main light source. A convenient little computer is available for working out these exposures.

Flash can also be used to create highlights where the natural light is flat, as on a very cloudy day. The flash can give a little kick or sparkle to what might otherwise be a dull-looking picture. The exposure can be computed in the same way as for the aquarium example.

Exposure Indexes

Some measure of the relative speed of films is necessary, obviously, for computing exposures. Exposure indexes are such a measure. They should not, however, be taken too seriously. The methods of arriving at these numbers are standardized within different countries where photographic products are made. The American system is called ASA after the American Standards Association. The British Standard (BS) is almost identical. The German system is called DIN, which stands for Deutsche Industrie Normen (and not, as some wags have suggested, for 'Das ist Normal'). The Japanese generally use American indexes.

E 2

A new system called Speed Value uses numbers from 1 to 10, usually written with a degree sign. These are part of an 'additive system for computing exposure' designed to simplify the arithmetic involved for those who can add but not multiply. The SV numbers are logarithms; a film of SV 7° is twice as fast as one of SV 6°. At the risk of sounding like an old fogey, I would suggest that those most likely to benefit from this 'improvement' will all be using automatic electric-eye cameras, anyway, before Speed Values are universally adopted.

All systems for rating the speed of films are based on a standard exposure and standard processing of the kind that most films get—that provided by the local chemist. Many professionals, whose films are developed individually, routinely use twice the standard exposure indexes for black-and-white. In colour, some films were found to function better at 1/3 to 1 stop over their ratings, others at less than rated speed. In 1960 the manufacturers issued new ratings for black-and-white films which are about double the previous speeds. This change is independent of any improvements in the film—it is merely the result of eliminating an unnecessary 'safety factor' in computing the speeds. The fact that the speeds could be changed by 100 per cent without markedly affecting the results should prove how relative they are.

Emulsions are changing rapidly these days, and it is important to check the instruction sheets that come packed with the film in order to keep abreast of the latest developments. For precise work, new films should be tested under controlled conditions *before* they are used for real picture-taking. The exposure indexes given by manufacturers are more realistic now than they used to be, but they still may need to be modified for a specific situation.

Actually, it is possible to get some kind of picture from any one of a wide range of exposures. For the very best picture, the exposure must be adjusted in some way to fit the nature of the subject and the quality of the light. Whether this is done by varying the film speed or by 'interpreting' the meter reading, the result will be the same. Subjects of high contrast will require more exposure than average; subjects of low contrast will need less.

These adjustments in exposure should be made even if the films will all receive the same development. Ideally, both exposure and development should be adjusted to suit the subject, but adjusting the exposure alone will still result in improvement.

Learning when and how to make these adjustments requires practice. The first step is to make several varied exposures of every picture subject that will stand still, and study the results carefully. You may well find that the best picture is not the one that is made 'by the book'.

5:

Light and Colour

THERE is an unfortunate tendency for inexperienced photographers to shoot with colour film before they have learned to use black-and-white. This is unfortunate because colour is the more difficult medium, both technically and artistically. It is always best to learn new things one step at a time, not so much for reasons of discipline as so that one can see some satisfying results early in the process and thus avoid getting discouraged too soon.

It should be remembered that even though the pictures may be in black-and-white, the subject is usually in colour, so the picture is always a translation of the original. The colours of the subject are represented in the picture either by shades of grey, if the picture is in black-and-white, or by shades of colour if the picture is in colour. In either case, the way that the colours are represented in the picture is called the 'rendering' of the colours. It is never 100 per cent 'accurate'.

The colours of the subject are never reproduced exactly in a colour photograph. Even if they were, they would not necessarily be *seen* as exactly the same, for reasons we will examine presently. But the rendering of colours is one of the factors that the photographer can control. It is part of his photographic language, and therefore it is one of the tools he must learn to use.

Although colour pictures are quite different from black-and-white pictures, the artistic differences are much greater than the mechanical differences. All photographic images are recorded on film in the same way—as lesser or greater concentrations of silver grains, which render the film more or less transparent after it is developed and fixed. This is true even if the film is colour film, because colour film does not record images in colour. It records a set of three black-and-white images, one on top of the other, corresponding more or less accurately to differently coloured components of the original scene. The colour we see when we look at the resulting picture is added later in processing. Even with films that yield positive transparencies the original images are black-and-white negatives and the processing not only adds colour but also converts the negative images to positive.

Since colour film is really an elaborate arrangement of black-and-white films, the two types of film behave in much the same way. For example, they are both sensitive to ultra-violet, which lies beyond the range of human vision. This fact is important in landscape photography, as we will see.

Colour film requires greater precision in exposure and processing than black-and-white film because it is more complicated. Using it also requires more understanding of how light and colour operate, but it is the artistic, rather than the technical complexity that makes it advisable to learn black-and-white first.

The usual reason given by inexperienced photographers for shooting in colour is that colour is easier to get processed and that colour slides are easier to display than prints. Neither of these is a good reason for shooting in colour. This is like deciding to paint a picture in water colours rather than oils because water colours dry more quickly. I am not convinced that colour processing is really available more widely than black-and-white processing, but I do not doubt that its quality is more uniform. Some people think that if they shoot black-and-white they ought to do their own processing; that seems like a lot of trouble, so they shoot colour and send the processing to a commercial laboratory with no qualms.

Similarly, the method of storage or exhibition does not really dictate the choice of colour or black-and-white. Either medium can produce slides or prints. While a slide show ensures a captive audience (if not a captivated one) there are also advantages to pictures that can be hung on the wall. Prints are easier to edit than transparencies, and negatives are easier to file. It is quite possible to make black-and-white pictures into slides, if that seems necessary. It is done routinely with illustrations for lectures and scientific papers. One trick that is often used is to copy black-and-white prints on reversal colour film (such as Kodachrome, Ektachrome, or Anscochrome) so that the film will automatically be developed into a positive and mounted for projection. This method is quick and relatively inexpensive, but better quality can be obtained with materials designed for black-and-white work, such as Fine Grain Positive film.

I suspect that one reason why people shoot in colour is that they consider it more 'realistic'. In a way, it is. But realism is not necessarily an advantage, and neither is colour, necessarily.

All forms of art make use of the imagination of the viewer. This is most apparent, perhaps, in the theatre, where we readily accept the idea that the stage is a heath or a submarine or whatever the playwright says it is. In literature, scenes that are merely sketched may have a stronger impact than those that are described in detail, and fashion designers know that suggestion is far stronger than revealed truth. The element of imagination is less obvious in photography, but just as powerful, and black-and-white is frequently more evocative than colour precisely because it is less 'realistic'.

There is no hard-and-fast barrier between a picture that is art and one that is information, and the fact that a picture is intended to be informative is no excuse for neglecting its artistic aspects. Actually, imagination plays as large a role in our understanding of facts as it does in our appreciation of art. Children demonstrate this when they act out whatever they are learning about; adults demonstrate it in reverse by the difficulty they have in learning about things that cannot easily be imagined, such as the destructiveness of modern weapons or the dimensions of outer space.

The choice of black-and-white or colour is, therefore, a fundamental one and should be made intelligently according to the scope and purpose of the photography.

It is technically possible to make acceptable black-and-white prints from positive colour originals, and with the newly-developed colour negative films it is not only possible but convenient to make either colour or black-and-white positives from the same negative. This achievement is most welcome, because it eliminates some of the need for using two cameras or changing film frequently. But although a colour picture may now be made on the same roll of film as a black-and-white picture, this does not mean that the photographer should approach them in the same way.

In colour there will often be elements affecting the composition that would not be important in black-and-white. Patches of identical colour, for example, will echo each other and may tie together different parts of the picture. There are contrasts in colour as well as between light and dark. In short, colour really does introduce another dimension in composition.

How Colours Are Seen

One of the reasons why colours cannot be reproduced accurately in colour pictures is that our perception of colours is variable. The appearance of a colour is influenced by its surroundings, the light falling on it, and by what we 'know' about it. A blue-green rectangle surrounded by green will look blue; if surrounded by blue the same rectangle will look green. The apparent brightness also will change according to the surroundings. Since the conditions under which we view the picture are seldom the same as those under which we viewed the subject, it is not surprising that the colours may not look the same.

More remarkable, however, is the ability of the eye to resist changes in the colour of objects caused by changing illumination. The most common illustration of this is provided by the shifting colours of daylight. A white sand beach will still look white in the late afternoon, when the light illuminating it is actually orange; it will also look white on a cloudy day when the light is rich in blue. This effect, known to psychologists as 'constancy', is produced entirely in the visual cortex of the viewer. It cannot be experienced by the film in a camera.

To appreciate the actual, physical differences in the colour of daylight from one time to another, it is necessary only to take colour photographs of the same scene at different times of day and compare the results. What will be seen on the film is what is actually there; what the eye sees is corrected to compensate for changes in the colour of the illumination.

Colour films are 'balanced' for one specific kind of light, 'daylight' films for the mixture of direct sun and reflected sky light encountered in the middle of the day in temperate latitudes, and 'indoor' film for one or another of the commonly used artificial light sources. Since films cannot 'correct' themselves as the eye does, they must be corrected by the photographer for any illumination at all different from that for which they were designed.

The Colour of Light

As we all know, 'white' daylight is made up of a mixture of wavelengths including the entire visible spectrum plus a bit of ultraviolet on one end and a bit of infra-red on the other. The proportions of the various wavelengths change with the weather and the time of day, but the complete range is there. A light source such as an incandescent lamp or a flash bulb is similar in that it has a *continuous spectrum*: the range of wavelengths that make up its light may not be as wide as in daylight, but within that range all are represented. There are no 'holes' in the spectrum.

The apparent colour of the light from such sources is measured in terms of 'colour temperature', which is the actual temperature (in degrees Kelvin) to which a standard 'black body' must be heated to give off light of the same apparent colour. The relationship between colour and temperature is recognized in our vernacular: 'white hot' is hotter than 'red hot.'

TABLE 2

Average colour temperatures of some common light sources

	°K	Note
Shadow areas in daylight (lighted by blue sky)	12,000	
Slight overcast sky	7,800	
Electronic flash (units vary)	6,600	
Noon sunlight on clear day	5,600	D
Sunlight in early morning or late afternoon	5,000	
Clear flash bulbs	3,800	F
Photoflood lamps	3,400	A
Studio floodlights	3,200	B
Household lamps, 75 watt and up	2,860	
Household lamps, up to 60 watt	2,760	

Notes

A. Light for which Type A films are balanced
B. Light for which Type B films are balanced
D. Light for which Daylight-type films are balanced
F. Light for which Type F films are balanced

It must be emphasized that these numbers describe only the appearance of the light; but appearance does not define the actual composition of the light. Two light sources may look the same even though their light is actually made up of different components. The same is true of colours.

Some light sources (the most common of which are fluorescent lamps) have discontinuous spectra, which means that some wavelengths are not represented at all in their output. Objects look reasonably natural to us under these lights because the eye is somehow able to supply the missing colours. Film, of course, has no such capacity to adapt. Colour photography with these light sources is unpredictable, but where tests can be made and evaluated in advance such lighting can be quite useful. One advantage of fluorescent lights is that they produce very little heat (infra-red is not included in their spectra). Another is that fluorescent tubes can be made in various shapes, including that of a doughnut, so that the light source can surround the lens (or the subject if it is small) to produce shadowless illumination. Colour temperature cannot be used to described the light such sources give.

At the extreme of the discontinuous-spectrum light sources are those that give off only one or a few narrow bands of wavelengths. Mercury vapour and sodium vapour lamps used for illuminating highways are the commonest examples of these sources. The distribution of wavelengths in their output is so meagre that not even the human eye can perceive colours under them—a fact that was brought home to the U.S. police when they discovered to their consternation that they could not identify the coloured registration plates of cars at night. Light sources of this type are called monochromatic. They are not, of course, suitable for colour photography but they have some specialized uses in black-and-white photography, which are discussed in Chapter 14.

What we define as 'white' or 'colourless' light is, of course, highly variable, ranging all the way from the light of a kerosene lamp to that of a carbon arc. White sunlight, as we know it, is sunlight that has had much of the blue filtered out of it by passing through our atmosphere. On the moon, where there is no atmosphere, the sky is black even in the daytime and the light arriving from the sun contains a higher proportion of blue, violet, and ultra-violet than on earth.

Filters and How They Work

The rendering of colours is controlled by the choice of film, the colour of the light and by filters. Filters are generally placed in front of the lens, although for some special purposes they are used over the light sources. In a few long lenses the filters are inserted between or behind the lens elements.

Filters absorb or 'block' certain wavelengths and transmit others. A filter may transmit a wide band of wavelengths or a narrow one, and the boundary between the absorbed and the transmitted wavelengths may be gradual or abrupt. It is impossible to tell from the appearance of the filter. For example, a red filter is one that appears red to the eye; it transmits red light and absorbs light of other colours to a greater or lesser degree. All filters that look red are red filters, but their optical characteristics may differ in ways that cannot be distinguished by the eye. Like light sources, filters may have widely differing characteristics and still look the same.

The action of filters is essentially the same with colour films as it is with black-and-white, since, as we have seen, all films operate on the same principle. But heavily coloured filters cannot be used with colour films because they impart an over-all cast to the picture. The great degree of control available in black-and-white through the use of filters cannot be matched in colour. This is an important advantage of black-and-white over colour.

A convenient example, because it is so familiar, is the problem of haze in distant landscapes. A certain amount of haze is always present, the amount varying with the location and the weather. The extent to which it appears in a picture can be, and is, controlled with filters. Complete control can be achieved only in black-and-white.

What is haze?

Haze is caused by minute particles of moisture and dust in the atmosphere that scatter some of the light coming from the sun, diverting it from its path. The scattering is selective; it is greatest at the blue end of the spectrum and least at the red end. Scattering is similar to the breaking up of 'white' light into spectral colours by drops of water to form a rainbow. A similar phenomenon occurs in snow, where the crystals scatter light in somewhat the same way. The light passing through snow becomes predominantly blue. The light inside snow caves is blue and so, although it is less obvious, are the shadows that reveal texture in masses of snow. The shadows will not photograph as shadows and the texture will be lost unless a filter is used to block some of the intense blue light and most of the ultra-violet that otherwise light up the shadows and make them look the same as the highlights to the film.

Some other colours in nature—notably those of the blue eyes of

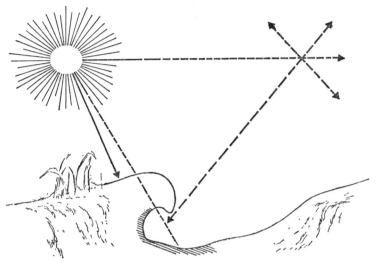

Fig. 11 Why shadows on snow are blue. The blue light is scattered by snow crystals and penetrates a snow bank. Other colours are absorbed or reflected by the snow. Shadow is also illuminated by blue light from the sky opposite the sun. Since film is highly sensitive to blue, shadows will disappear on film unless a filter is used.

babies and the plumage of bluebirds—are also produced by scattering.

It is scattering that accounts for the blue appearance of the sky and also for the red colour of the setting sun, as we shall see. The ultra-violet, violet, and blue are scattered the most as they pass through the atmosphere. They are reflected down toward the earth, thus imparting their colours to the sky, especially that part of the sky opposite the sun. It is as though the sky were a giant mirror which could reflect only blue light. Looking at it we would see it as blue. The orange, red, and infra-red pass through the atmosphere with much less scattering. Consequently they are not seen in that part of the sky that is lighted only by scattered light (they pass though the mirror).

When we look at the sun we see all the colours, because all pass through the atmosphere, but some of the blue is removed before the light reaches us. When the sun is low in the sky, however, it is seen through a much greater thickness of atmosphere than when

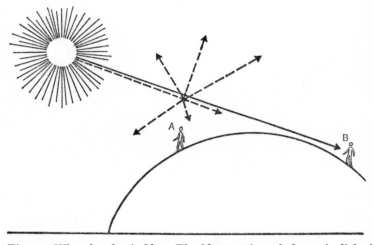

Fig. 12 Why the sky is blue. The blue portion of the sun's light is scattered by particles in the atmosphere. Observer A sees it as blue sky. To him, the sun appears white. For Observer B, the sun is setting and he sees it through a greater thickness of atmosphere than A. To him, the sun is red because the blue rays do not reach him.

it is overhead. The thickness is so great near the horizon that not only the blue rays but also much of the green and yellow are scattered before they reach us, and all that remain are the orange and red parts of the spectrum. That is why the setting sun looks red. The missing blue rays, meanwhile, are reflected down to earth as 'sky light' farther around the earth's circumference where it is still day.

When the density of moisture and dust particles in the air is extreme (as in New York in the summer or Los Angeles at any time of year) the scattering encompasses other colours as well as blue and the appearance of blueness in the sky is lost. Even in a heavy fog 'warm' colours are scattered less than 'cool' ones. This is why yellow fog lights are used on cars. The part of the haze that consists of solid particles of dust or soot is not, of course, transparent to light of any colour, but it does interfere more with the blues and violets because it scatters them to a greater extent than the reds.

Distant scenes on earth have a 'washed out' appearance because

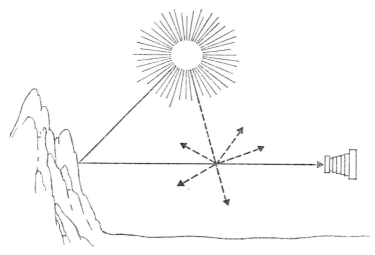

Fig. 13 The effect of haze. Blue light and ultra-violet, scattered by haze between the camera and its distant subject, makes the scene look washed out. The effect on film is even greater, unless filters are used, because the film is more sensitive to blue than is the eye.

the atmosphere through which they are seen and photographed scatters blue light and ultra-violet like a smoke screen and this scattered light, coming from *in front* of the subject, obscures our view. The effect is more apparent on film (either black-and-white or colour) than it is to the eye because ultra-violet, to which the film is sensitive but the human eye is not, is scattered even more than blue light. In black-and-white this U-V appears as extra light and reduced contrast. Colour film records it as a washed-out bluish haze.

As we have seen, red and orange wavelengths of light penetrate the atmosphere with less difficulty than blue ones. Therefore if we are to photograph a distant scene, we would expect to achieve increased clarity by restricting the response of the film to the reddish wavelengths. This is what happens in actual practice. It is not always desirable, however, to eliminate haze completely since it is one of the cues that enable us to 'see' depth. Obviously the distance between our two eyes is so small that the difference between their two images cannot have much effect on depth perception at distances of several miles, but we are accustomed to the progressive 'greying' of colours and softening of contrasts as distance increases (called 'atmospheric perspective' in painting) and we accept these cues as indicators of distance. People arriving for the first time in the mountains, where the air is extremely clear, consistently underestimate distances.

With black-and-white film we have almost complete control over the amount of haze visible in the photograph. We can *increase* the apparent haze by using only the blue end of the spectrum. We could achieve this by taking the picture through a blue filter, thus reducing the effect of the other colours and accentuating the scattered wavelengths.

With no filter, the haze would still be heavier in the picture than it appears to the eye, due to the ultra-violet and other differences in sensitivity between the eye and the film.

The scene could be shown approximately as it appears to the eye by photographing it through a medium yellow filter.

For greater haze penetration, an orange filter could be used.

Next, with panchromatic black-and-white film (orthochromatic not being in general use now), a red filter could be used, then a darker red.

Then, for absolute clarity, we could change to infra-red-sensitive film and use a filter that would exclude virtually all visible light, thus exposing the film only to infra-red, which is not scattered by the atmosphere at all. (This is one of the techniques used in aerial photography and makes it possible to photograph through clouds.)

With each step, the exposure must be increased because a smaller proportion of the total light is being used.

Also with each step, the sky would become darker as a greater proportion of the blue sky light is prevented by the filter from reaching the film. There are other changes, too, making the picture

[7] *Scottish landscape. Backlighting reveals contours; haze shows depth.*

Left [8] *A boll weevil, photographed in the laboratory with high-speed electronic flash. (See page 98.)*

Right [9] *Otters are among the most photogenic of animals. This one was photographed in the New York Zoo. A large aperture was used to throw the background out of focus (see page 157).*

look progressively less natural. In the final case, using only infra-red, foliage will appear white and the sky black.

As a rule of thumb, any filter will lighten objects of its own colour and darken those of complementary hue. In addition to the blue, yellow, orange, and red filters just described, there are a few more specialized types used with black-and-white film. One of the most useful is a light green, which can be used to make foliage appear lighter and also to darken the sky without lightening skin tones when people are photographed outdoors.

In colour photography, the control available by the use of filters is limited because filtering can throw the colour off balance. Let us try photographing the same distant landscape in colour.

With no filter, the colour film, like the black-and-white, will record more haze than the eye can see because of the film's sensitivity to ultra-violet. We can correct the sensitivity of the film to approximate that of the eye by blocking the ultra-violet with a 'Skylight', 'Haze', or 'U-V' filter. (Since most of the wavelengths they block are invisible to us, these filters appear almost colourless. They do not ordinarily require any increase in exposure.)

An orange filter would give greater haze penetration, as it does in black-and-white, but it would colour the entire scene orange. There is one solution—use a film balanced for warmer (more orange) light, together with the appropriate orange filter, called a conversion or light-balancing filter, that adapts it for use with daylight. There is one of these for each type of 'artificial light' film. It is not generally known that they also subdue haze. Of course, they are not as dark as the filters used with black-and-white. The filters used in colour photography do not block *all* of a colour, they merely absorb some of it to correct the balance among the colours. It is a convenience to say that an orange filter adds orange, but what it actually does is to subtract other colours.

How Colour Films Work

Sir Isaac Newton discovered that if the solar spectrum (such as that thrown by a prism, see Fig. 14) was bent into a circle with the colours which are not in the spectrum but nevertheless visible—the purples and magentas—inserted between the violet and red ends, where they seem to belong, then every colour would fall

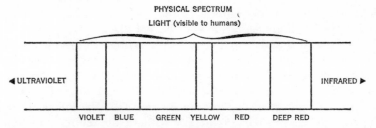

Fig. 14 *The physical spectrum. Light lies between ultra-violet and infra-red. Most films respond to light and the near ultra-violet. Specialized films respond to some infra-red. The visible portion of the spectrum is represented on colour film.*

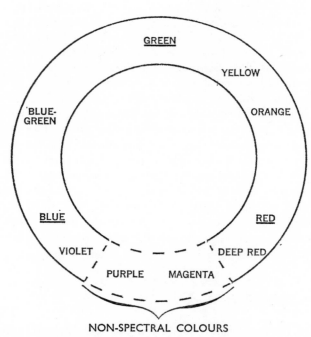

Fig. 15A *How colours are represented in colour photography. The visible spectrum (light) plus the non-spectral colours (purple and magenta) are represented as a circle. Colours that are opposite each other on the circle are complementary.*

opposite its complementary colour (Fig. 15A). Any pair of complementary colours if mixed together in equal amounts would cancel each other and produce a neutral tone.

There are two ways of mixing colours. If coloured lights are mixed, as when differently coloured spotlights are aimed at the same wall, the colours are added together and the result is called an 'additive' mixture. The additive mixture of all the colours in

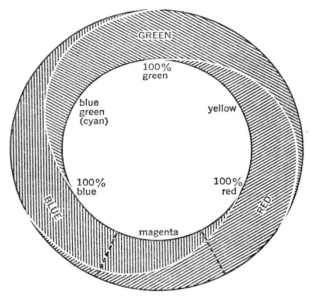

Fig. 15B *On colour film, all the colours in* 15A *are recorded as various combinations of three primaries.*

sunlight produces 'white' light. Additive mixture of any pair of complementaries will also produce white.

On the other hand, pigments and filters function by absorbing some colours from the light and reflecting or transmitting others. When pigments are mixed, or filters superimposed, each one subtracts some colours from the light. Such a mixture is called 'subtractive'. The subtractive mixture of all colours yields black; so does the subtractive mixture of any pair of complementaries.

Colours have another, even more remarkable property: any *three* colours that are sufficiently separated on the circle can, by additive mixture, produce all the other colours. The only absolute restriction on the choice of colours for such mixture is that no two of them can be complementary.

It is this fact that makes colour photography and colour printing possible. All the various colours and shadings of a subject are recorded on colour film as different proportions of three primary colours. The primaries used in colour photography are blue, green, and red. As was mentioned earlier, colour films record their images in black-and-white; the colour is added later in processing.

TABLE 3

Primary colours used in colour photography
and their mixtures

ADDITIVE MIXTURE (mixing light)

Additive Primaries are Red, Green, and Blue

Red *plus* Blue	*equals*	Magenta
Blue *plus* Green	*equals*	Cyan (Blue-green)
Green *plus* Red	*equals*	Yellow
Green *plus* Red *plus* Blue	*equals*	White

Therefore:

Magenta *plus* Green	*equals*	White
Cyan *plus* Red	*equals*	White
Yellow *plus* Blue	*equals*	White

SUBTRACTIVE MIXTURE (superimposing filters)

Subtractive Primaries are Magenta, Cyan, and Yellow
(Each of these primaries is the sum of *two* of the additive primaries)

Yellow *minus* Magenta	*equals*	Red
Cyan *minus* Magenta	*equals*	Blue
Yellow *minus* Cyan	*equals*	Green
Cyan *minus* Magenta *minus* Yellow	*equals*	Black

Therefore:

Cyan *minus* Red	*equals*	Black
Yellow *minus* Blue	*equals*	Black
Magenta *minus* Green	*equals*	Black

The difference between a colour film and a black-and-white film is that the colour film has three emulsion layers 'stacked' on one base, whereas black-and-white film ordinarily has only one layer. Each of the three layers is sensitive to light of one of the three primary colours. The top layer is sensitive only to blue, the middle layer to green, and the bottom layer to red. Since all emulsions are inherently sensitive to blue, a yellow dye is inserted under the blue-sensitive top layer to prevent blue light from reaching the green-sensitive and red-sensitive layers below. This dye dissolves in processing (Fig. 16).

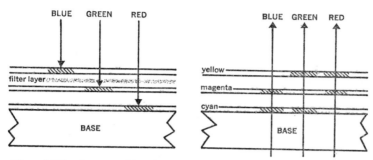

Fig. 16 The three emulsion layers of colour film (left) record blue, green, and red light respectively. A yellow dye is put between the blue and green layers to prevent blue light from reaching the lower two emulsions. In processing, the layer of dye dissolves and the three layers are dyed yellow, magenta, and cyan respectively, with the result that the light passing through the positive transparency is the same colour as that which made the original exposure (right).

When the film is processed into a positive transparency, the images in the three layers are reversed from negative to positive and the layers are dyed to re-create the colours. The dyes are complementaries of the original primaries: yellow, magenta, and cyan (a blue-green). At any point where a layer was fully exposed, no dye is deposited in that layer. Where a blue sky, for example, appeared in the original scene, the yellow dye will be absent from the emulsion layer that was originally sensitive to blue. The other two layers are dyed magenta (which passes red and blue but blocks green) and cyan (which passes blue and green but blocks red). The light passing through these two layers will have the green and red subtracted from it, leaving only blue. In this manner the light that passes through a transparency (or that reflected from a colour print) at any point will be the same colour as the light that fell on that point during the original exposure.

If we want to reduce the exposure in one layer, the way to do it is to use a filter that will block light of the colour to which that layer is sensitive. If, on the other hand, we want to increase the exposure in that layer, the only way a filter can do it is by blocking the colours of light to which the other two layers are sensitive. For this reason there are two types of filters for each layer in the colour film. They might be thought of as negative—that is, those which reduce the exposure in that layer—and positive—those which increase the relative exposure in that layer by reducing the exposure in the other two layers. The negative filters are cyan, magenta, and yellow, blocking red, green, and blue light, respectively; the positive filters are red, blue, and green. Each of these colours is available in six or seven densities or degrees of darkness, making a total of 40 filters all together.

The complete set of 40 would give almost total control over the rendering of colours. Only four or five of them are ordinarily needed for any one type of picture-taking. For example, only the red and magenta filters would be needed under water.

In addition to the basic filters, there are a number of special ones for specific purposes. They provide, for that particular situation, all the necessary corrections for all three layers in one filter, thus eliminating the necessity for a 'pack' of filters and reducing the loss of light that is inevitable when a number of filters are used together. Such special-purpose filters include those designed to alter the sensitivity of specific films to match certain light sources different from those for which they were designed, and filters that produce an over-all 'warming' or 'cooling' effect to correct daylight films for conditions other than noon sunlight on a clear day, the standard for which daylight films are balanced.

With negative colour films, corrections can be made in the process of making the positive print or transparency. This is usually more convenient than making them at the camera when the film is exposed. For this reason, negative colour films are not made to match as great a variety of light sources as reversal films. The degree of control available is one of the advantages of colour negative film. Among the other advantages are the possibility of making colour transparencies, colour prints, black-and-white prints, or printing plates all from the same negative, and the ease with which these can be enlarged or reduced in size. Areas in the picture can be made lighter or darker (as is done in black-and-white printing) and if the positive is in colour, the colour of various areas in the print can also be locally adjusted. Another advantage is that an entire roll of film can be contact printed on one sheet of colour or black-and-white paper as a proof, and the frames to be enlarged or printed can be selected from the proof. Filing the negatives and proofs is as simple as it is in black-and-white.

Even negative colour, however, cannot be corrected for more than one colour of light in any one picture. While light sources need not be matched to the film, as they must with reversal films, all the light sources used in any one picture must match each other in colour temperature.

The three-colour system of recording colours was developed because it was found by experience that all the colours we could see could be approximated by mixtures of three primaries. For the same reason it was long believed that there were three receptor systems in the eye that must function somewhat like the layers of film, although no one was ever able to confirm this hypothesis by actual experiment.

Recent research by Dr. Edwin Land suggests that three primaries are not necessary to produce a full range of colour sensation. Land divided the light coming from a collection of coloured objects into *two* images, corresponding merely to the longer and shorter wavelengths. The two images were then projected on to the same screen, one on top of the other. One of these images was projected through a red filter; the other with no filter at all. The resulting picture appeared in full colour! Land found that the dividing line between the two sets of wavelengths could be varied over a wide range without affecting the result, and that full colour could be seen even when the band of wavelengths admitted to each of the films was very narrow. The effect occurs only when the mixture is additive, that is, when *light* is mixed. As yet it has no known applications, but it demonstrates that the eye is capable of reconstructing full colour from the scantiest of clues.

The more we learn about colour, the more of it seems to be in the eye of the beholder. It is not so surprising, then, that 'true' rendering of colours in photographs has proven so elusive a goal.

If a photograph is taken under controlled conditions, such that the photograph and the object held side by side under the same illumination will appear the same colour, there is still no assurance that they will appear the same colour under any other illumination. Fortunately, the adaptation process in vision allows us to accept considerable deviation from the 'real' colour of objects before they begin to look unnatural.

Most people tend to describe colour rendering that they like as 'natural', but there may be considerable variation between observers in what they prefer. In one experiment a large number of people were shown a series of colour photographs that differed only in the 'warmth' of the colours. At one end of the scale the red and orange tones were predominant; at the other end the blues were emphasized. The subjects were asked to select the most 'pleasing' rendering. Women subjects selected a 'cooler' rendering, on the average, than men. Undoubtedly these subjects, being untrained observers, felt that the most 'pleasing' picture was also the most 'accurate'.

Thus it is fairly well established that 'accurate' rendering of colours is really impossible in a photograph. Even if the reproduction is controlled to the photographer's complete satisfaction, there is no assurance that another viewer would agree. In fact, we have no real way of knowing that another viewer even sees the same colours we do! People frequently live normal lives for years before discovering accidentally that they are partially colour blind.

Polarity of Light

Light has other characteristics, some of them invisible to humans, that are useful in photography. Polarity is one of them. Light vibrates in various planes, and the light from an ordinary source such as the sun or an incandescent lamp vibrates at random in all planes that are perpendicular to the path of the light. The light rays vibrating in these various planes differ in their polarity and although they all look the same to us, they do not all behave in the same way. For example, they reflect differently. When light hits a shiny surface like the surface of a lake, the rays that vibrate in a horizontal plane tend to bounce off, while those vibrating in a vertical plane are more likely to penetrate the surface.

Light that has been filtered so that all its rays vibrate in the same direction is said to be polarized. In nature, different kinds of light may be polarized to different degrees. The reflections from the surface of the lake are partly polarized, as are the rays reflected from below the surface that permit us to see into the water. The most efficient polarizer in nature is the sky; sunlight is not polarized but light reflected from the sky at right angles to the sun is strongly polarized. Bees are able to see the polarity of light and make use of

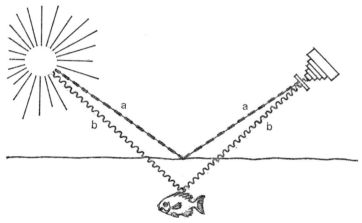

Fig. 17 Polarity of light. Light vibrating in a horizontal plane (a) tends to be reflected from a horizontal surface such as that of a pond. Light vibrating in a vertical plane (b) tends to penetrate the horizontal surface. The polarities may be separated by a filter, reducing reflections from the surface of the pond and revealing objects beneath. The effect is greatest at an angle of 35° to the surface.

that ability to find their way to and from the hive. They can detect polarity even on cloudy days when the sun is hidden. Photographers can also make use of polarity by introducing filters that pass only light vibrating in one selected plane.

In photographing the lake mentioned above, we might choose to emphasize the surface reflections. We could make them more apparent in the picture than they are to the eye by using a polarizer at the camera to ensure that only light vibrating in a horizontal plane would reach the film. On the other hand, we could reduce the reflections and make objects beneath the surface more easily visible by turning the polarizer so as to reject horizontal vibrations and admit vertical ones.

Light that is already polarized can be controlled by a polarizing filter, while unpolarized light is unaffected. Because the reflections from the surface of the lake are polarized horizontally while those from beneath the surface are polarized vertically, we can separate them with the polarizer. The filter has an indicating mark, usually an arrow, on its edge to indicate the plane of vibration it will pass, so we can tell which way it is set. In the same fashion, we can control the light from that part of the sky that reflects polarized light. Polarity has nothing to do with the colour of light, so a polarizing filter can be used with colour film to darken the sky without affecting the rendering of other colours in the scene.

We can also create polarized light of our own, by placing polarizing filters in the path of the light. This is often done in the studio to control reflections, especially in copying.

If the polarization of light were 100 per cent complete and the efficiency of the polarizing filter were likewise 100 per cent, then the filter would pass 100 per cent of the light when it was aligned with the plane of the light. When the polarity of the filter was at right-angles to the polarity of the light, no light would pass through it and it would appear black. In actual practice, none of these values is 100 per cent but a very large degree of control is still possible. And although the theoretical polarizer would have no effect on colours, the actual filters available (like most glass) do block out ultra-violet.

Because a polarizer will pass different proportions of the light reaching it, depending on the extent to which the light is polarized and the angle of the polarizer, it is not possible to tell exactly how much exposure-increase the polarizer will require. In daylight, the polarizer will normally block at least half of the light that will be measured by a meter. Surface reflections tend, in any case, to make a meter give false high readings because they act like light sources. For these reasons, the average exposure increase (over the exposure indicated by meter) when using a polarizer is four times or two stops. When possible, exposures made with a polarizer should be 'bracketed'; that is, a series of exposures, differing by one stop in black-and-white or one half stop in colour, should be made, with the two-stop increase as the midpoint. An accurate exposure could be determined with a specialized meter sensitive enough to read the intensity of the actual image on a ground glass, or with on-the-spot tests made on Polaroid film.

Summary

The various characteristics of light and film are used by the photographer to control the results of his picture-taking. Although they may be used to make the picture look more like the subject, complete 'accuracy' is not possible. This fact need not be a source of despair to the photographer; rather it should strengthen his adherence to the creative process. The photograph is an object in itself—an object of beauty, we hope—and *not* a reproduction of nature. His control over colour is one of the tools that the photographer uses to create this new independent object. Thus, while it is not possible for the photographer to reproduce colours exactly, it is important for him to know how to render them as he desires.

6:

Creative Controls

IN the foregoing chapters we have discussed the major technical means by which the photographer can make his picture look the way he wants it to look. The most important are:

Perspective, controlled by viewpoint.
Image size, controlled by lens focal length.
Depth of field, controlled by lens aperture.
Motion-stopping power, controlled by shutter speed.
The appearance of light, controlled by exposure.
Contrast, controlled by lighting, exposure, and development.
Rendering of colour, controlled by filters.
Reflections, controlled (sometimes) by polarization.

Composition

The most important non-technical control is composition. It is not, of course, peculiar to photography but functions in the same way in all pictures, regardless of the medium in which they are created. A mosaic, an etching, a photograph, and a *collage* could all, conceivably, be composed in the same way.

Composition has become so surrounded by mystery that it may be safer to call it 'organization'. It includes so simple a thing as deciding whether to put a subject in the centre of the picture or at one side, or whether to place a rectangle parallel to the edge of the picture or at an angle. On a more complex level it involves the balancing of masses and the use of lines to control the centre of interest.

Every picture has composition, good or bad. Composition means simply the way that the parts of the image are organized into a picture. A well-composed picture is said to 'hold together'; a poorly composed one to 'fall apart'. In a well-composed picture the subject 'stands out'; in a poorly composed one it is 'lost'. Composition is part of a visual language that is largely learned and becomes largely unconscious. One of the sources from which we learn composition is nature, and that is why nature often appears so well composed to us. Another source of learning is the visual culture around us and this, of course, is not the same for all people in all times and places. Presumably a photographer brought up in the tradition of Islamic art would compose pictures differently from a European photographer. (We know that this is true of painters.) Sometimes there are even detectable differences between photographs by English, French, Swiss, and Japanese photographers although they are all products of a fairly uniform visual culture these days, and differences are visible only occasionally.

Composition can be learned, but not by rote. It is not immutable, and while it may have conventions, it does not have laws. The 'laws of composition', involving such things as S curves and locating the centre of interest one third of the distance from edge to edge of the picture, are crutches for the lame-brained. They were invented by a group of amateur photographers who called themselves 'pictorialists' because they imitated paintings. They held sway within camera clubs during the first half of the twentieth century, where they conducted contests called 'salons' and awarded tin trinkets to one another. By now most of them have died off, leaving no trace upon photography in general except the loss of some potentially talented people whom they scared away.

Composition is a matter of taste, and thus cannot be governed by rules. But although we cannot tell anyone how to achieve good taste, we can tell the difference between good and bad. *De gustibus non disputandam* does not mean that there can be no agreement on matters of taste; it merely means that it is useless to try to explain them. The content of a picture is like the words of a song. It can be explained, more or less, in words. The form of the picture, however, is like the music of the song. It can not really be explained; it has to be experienced.

Processing

Most of the creative control available to the photographer is applied before the exposure is made. The remainder is exercised in processing. The greatest flexibility is available in black-and-white;

the least in colour reversal films. Colour negative film is inter-mediate; it permits a degree of control in processing colour pictures that approaches what we have always enjoyed in black-and-white.

Should a photographer develop and print his own pictures? This question has provoked reams of highly theoretical and sometimes highly emotional argument, most of it from those who take the affirmative. The gist of their position seems to be that for the photographer to do his own darkroom work is morally good (like physical fitness), and that there is something dishonest about a picture that was taken by one man and printed by another.

Most professionals simply cannot afford to make their own prints, and many admit frankly that the printers who do their work can do it not only cheaper, but also better than they can. Depending on his affluence and volume of work, a professional may maintain his own darkroom with his own technician (often a man he has trained himself) or he may use one of the laboratories in metropolitan centres that cater to professionals. If he works for an institution or publication, they may maintain a darkroom. The ordinary mass-production photo-finishers that do work for chemists and dealers are just not equipped for quality.

I think there is very little question that a man who spends his entire time printing can, if he has talent, develop more skill, and certainly more speed, than a man who divides his working time between printing and picture-taking. On the other side, the photographer supposedly 'knows exactly what he wants'. Actually, the chief advantage of photographer-printing is that, if he doesn't know what he wants, he can experiment, as a professional printer seldom can, and try different ways of printing the picture before selecting the one he likes best.

But this is something different from regular picture-taking; it is a part of the photographer's training, a working out of problems and an aid to 'thinking through'. Clearly, it cannot be done by anyone else. There is also an occasional salvage operation where the picture-taking conditions prevented the photographer from making the picture the way he wanted it. In such a case, he may be better equipped than the printer to decide what compromises should be made to get a passable print.

But in general I think that skill in printing is neither an advan-tage nor a disadvantage to a photographer; it is merely irrelevant. The ability to memorize scores does not make one a symphony conductor; neither does the ability to make beautiful prints make one a photographer. It does not indicate anything about the ability to take pictures. The real test of a photographer is his ability to *see* pictures.

I have not found it hard to get across to a good printer how I want a picture to look. In most cases the simple markings used in editing contact prints are enough: a series of circles means 'make lighter', a row of squiggles means 'darken', and boundaries drawn on the contact indicate cropping. In the occasional instance where these instructions are not enough, a short conference with the printer will usually suffice.

At different times various contests have had various rules about the making of prints. In some the photographer must have made the print himself; for others it must have been made 'under his direction'; or, for others, if he didn't make the print himself he must certify that he is capable of doing so. These requirements sound pretty silly, and they are, but they reflect the uncertainty and lack of conviction of the old guard. There was a time when photographers had to know how to do darkroom work, and when the ability to develop and print was the cachet of the photographer as the ability to box the compass was of the mariner. That time was long, long ago. Incidentally, no one has suggested that there is anything unethical about letting an outside laboratory process one's colour transparencies.

There are several good reasons why a beginner should *not* do his own processing. A time when one is trying to learn how to take pictures is not a good time to learn processing as well. There are too many variables. If a picture is unsatisfactory, the inexperienced photographer has no way of knowing whether the fault is in the exposure or the processing, or both. He can go around and around and is likely to become discouraged too soon. The less experienced a photographer is, the more he needs standardized processing of his film in order to learn how changes in picture-taking variables affect the result.

The question of cost is a complicated one. It is very hard to say whether doing one's own processing is less expensive or more expensive than sending it out. It all depends on the volume, the quality of the darkroom installation, and whether the photographer has anything else to do with his time.

The decisive argument, it seems to me, is on the question of darkroom equipment. Processing, especially film developing and colour work, is not really so simple as the advertisements claim. To do a consistently good job you need an installation such as few

Fig. 18 *Marks used in editing photographs. The circles mean 'make lighter', the squiggles mean 'make darker'. Straight boundaries indicate exact cropping, squiggly boundaries indicate approximate croppings.*

beginners can afford. The temperature of processing solutions and even of the wash water should be precisely controlled. In many places the water supply needs to be filtered to remove invisible specks of dirt that can produce a mottling effect in

[10] *Fruit of mangrove will fall into water and float until it strikes bottom, then takes root*

[11] *Blossoms of moss plant,* Cassiope hypnoides, *cascade down a rock near the summit of Mount Washington. Like most alpine flowers, they are tiny.*

[12] *Tiny white or pink-tinged alpine bilberry,* Vaccinium uliginosum L., *grows on wind-swept slopes above timber line. Photograph is larger than life size.*

[13] *Lizard basking on a leaf is revealed by his shadow. (See page 155.)*

[14] *Two species of Daddy-longlegs, photographed in a dry aquarium. Background is a white card.*

shadow areas of negatives. In any climate where the temperature and humidity reach uncomfortable levels, darkrooms must be air-conditioned—not so much for the comfort of those who work there as to protect film against absorbing too much moisture from the air, or too many fingerprints from sweat-soaked fingers. The air in which film is dried must not be too damp, or the film will dry too slowly and the emulsion will swell, reducing the sharpness of the image. The drying air must not be too dry, either, or it will cause the film to curl and warp. Enlargers must be mounted so as to be absolutely free from vibration, and the air in the darkroom should be free of dust. It is possible, with the right machinery, to control all these factors, but obviously few beginning photographers are in a position to do so.

For these reasons, I think it is clearly an advantage for the beginning photographer to send his processing work to a good laboratory. How can he find one? One way would be to ask the editors of some publications that print consistently good pictures. Another might be to ask some of the photographers whose work he admires. Local camera dealers are sometimes reliable, sometimes not.

Good laboratories, for reasons of self-preservation, are usually located in cities where there is commercial activity in photography and printing. The photographer who lives elsewhere should not be deterred by the necessity of sending his film away. If he has been taking it to a local camera dealer or chemist the chances are that they have been sending it to the city anyway.

The best way to identify a good laboratory is to look at some of their work. Another way is this: If they ask you how the film was exposed when you bring it in, you can assume that they are equipped to suit the development to the shooting conditions.

Editing

One important way that the photographer exercises creative control over his results is through editing. The selection and arrangement of picture elements begins before the picture is taken, but does not end there. The choice of pictures, the cropping, and the changes in emphasis produced by printing, all contribute materially to the photograph's ability to communicate.

The experienced photographer seldom takes *one* picture of anything. If he photographs a subject at all, he takes a variety of pictures. Some will be vertical, some horizontal. Some will be close-ups, some long shots. He may use different lenses or filters. All of these pictures may be good, but they are only the raw material of the editing process. One of them will ultimately be chosen as the best—not best in any abstract sense, but best for the particular purpose at hand.

There are other reasons, too, for taking many photographs of one subject. In pictures of subjects that move, especially small ones, it may be impossible to be sure whether the subject was caught at an instant when it was still. And when photographing a wild animal a wise photographer will start taking pictures while still at a distance and keep on shooting as he moves closer. At some point the animal will decide he is close enough, and will move away. The photographer shoots each picture in the knowledge that it may be the last he will get, while hoping that the animal will let him get closer.

In many other situations, the experienced photographer will start with a picture that is less than ideal and will gradually 'zero-in' as far as the situation permits. Sometimes the situation develops unpredictably while it is being photographed. The photographer cannot know what will happen or which of the pictures he takes will be the most relevant ones.

Editors who hire photographers find that they can judge a man's ability best by looking at his complete 'take' on one story. A sheaf of contact prints, proofs of perhaps 200 frames, will tell an experienced editor much more than a portfolio of selected samples. They show how the photographer approaches a subject, experiments with different interpretations, and develops the one or ones he prefers. In short, they show how he thinks.

Photographers who work for publication have the advantage of working with editors and art directors in the selection and layout of their work. I am aware that many of them do not look upon this collaboration as an advantage, but I still think it is one. The photographer does not see his pictures with an outsider's eye. For him, the pictures have associations that they cannot have for someone seeing them for the first time. They trigger the photographer's recollection (indeed, that is precisely the function of many non-professional photographs) and he may see in them things that are really not there but in his memory. In editing for an outside audience, four eyes are better than two.

The purpose of the photography determines how photographs are edited. We have mentioned one frequently encountered purpose—to spark the photographer's memory. This is the function of most vacation and family-album pictures. It is a perfectly valid use of photography, but it explains why such photographs do not have the meaning for other people that they have for the participants.

Some other purposes of photography are:

to study the subject
to teach others about the subject
to convey an aesthetic experience
to portray the photographer's reaction to the subject
to display the photographer's virtuosity

A photograph may, of course, serve several purposes at once. In fact, that is one of the marks of a truly superior photograph.

How best to edit a set of pictures also depends on what use will be made of them. The photograph that would be chosen for the cover of a magazine might not be suitable to illustrate an article inside the magazine; the cover requires a more 'posterish' or 'graphic' picture—one that can be comprehended from a distance. Similarly, a picture to be hung on the wall or made into a mural would differ from one to be printed in a folder.

The difference between a fair photograph and a good one is very great, but it is very hard to explain. There is a similar difference between photographers who are good and those few who are really great. Imitators have spent years trying to figure out what the difference is, but there is still lots of room at the top. The same is true, of course, in all the other arts.

Ultimately, I think, the mark of a good photograph is its ability to communicate. This communication occurs on various levels. It can be factual, it can be aesthetic, it can be emotional. If the photography is *very* good, it will communicate on all these levels at once, and each aspect will reinforce the other.

If the ability to communicate is the test of a good photograph, then it follows that the means by which the photograph will reach its audience is an inseparable part of the artistic process. An unseen photograph is like an unheard piece of music;

G 2

philosophically it may not even exist. A photograph cannot be 'good' in a vacuum; it must be considered in relation to how it will be used. Editing, which is the process of making the photograph fit the use, is therefore a step in the creative process.

It is no excuse for the lazy photographer to claim that a photograph is 'just a record'. A record of what? It is clearly impossible for a photograph to be a record of everything that occurred at a certain time and place. There is some selection, inevitably, and selection is the most important artistic element in photography. If the photograph is a record of the appearance of something, it must record the appearance of it *to* someone. There is no escape from this subjective element. All human beings frequently do less than their best, but we cannot cover up our lapses by shifting the responsibility to the subject.

What it is that the photograph communicates will depend on what the photographer puts into it, and that depends largely on his willingness to learn from his subjects. Photographs are made by people, not by machines. They are personal, not objective. Anyone who still believes that 'pictures don't lie' should look at *The Americans*, a book by a young Swiss photographer, Robert Frank.

It has been said that there are only two kinds of photography—good and bad. Actually, I think, many photographs are hard to classify in one of those categories and certainly photographs can be categorized in other ways as well. For example, there is 'warm' photography and 'cool' photography. These are the best names I can think of to describe photographs in which the emotional element is more or less important—photographs that contain different degrees of emotion. I am not sure that one is better than the other; they are simply different.

Explaining the difference between good photographs and not-so-good ones is difficult for everyone. That is why people so often take refuge in technical talk about things like grain and sharpness. They may not be relevant, but they are concrete. People are made uncomfortable by uncertainty. If they do not know whether a picture is good or not they will talk instead about the ferrotyping of the print. The photographer who wants to develop his skill should not ignore technique, but he should not worship it either.

He should always remember that technique is a tool. It can be used to make masterpieces or to turn out junk, depending on who uses it and how.

Part Two

APPLICATIONS

7 °°

Landscapes and Plants

WE have all seen landscapes in nature so impressive that it seemed that any picture we might take of them would be bound to be a masterpiece. When we got home and looked at the pictures, however, they didn't look grand at all. Everything was so tiny and far away!

There are several reasons why the picture does not look like the scene. They all come down to the fact that when we look at it, we are looking at a *picture* and not at a real landscape. In other words, the viewing conditions are not comparable.

Let us take as an example one of these spectacular sunsets that usually prove so disappointing in a photograph. In Chapter 5 we discussed how scattering of light accounts for the colour of the blue sky and also for the redness of the setting sun. It does not, however, account for the setting sun's apparent size. The actual size of the sun (or moon) is the same when it is near the horizon as when it is high in the sky, and photographs will show it that way. But when an observer looks at the sun, he sees it as about one third larger on the horizon than overhead.

This phenomenon, which is known as the moon illusion, is the most striking example of how the mind 'corrects' what the eye sees, and it demonstrates the impossibility of reproducing in a photograph the visual effect of looking at an actual scene.

In the second century A.D., Ptolemy noted the moon illusion and suggested an explanation of it. After the dawn of experimental psychology, the moon illusion became a popular subject for research. Experimental subjects looked at the moon through prisms, filters, and masks; they looked at it sitting, standing, lying down, and bending over to look between their legs. They compared the moon with discs of cardboard and spots of light projected, in one experiment, on the interior of a zeppelin hangar, and more recently on half-silvered mirrors through which the real sky could be seen.

These researches suggest that Ptolemy's explanation is substantially correct: When the moon is on the horizon it looks larger

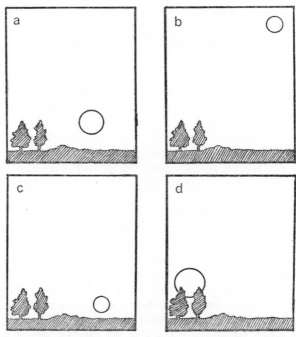

Fig. 19 *Why a landscape picture does not look like the actual landscape. In vision, images are 'corrected' for what the observer believes the size and distance of the object to be. The moon illusion* (above) *is the most obvious example. When seen near the horizon* (a) *the moon appears larger than when it is seen overhead* (b). *Its actual size, and that seen in a photograph* (c), *is the same at any elevation. The effect is increased if the moon is seen 'framed' by foreground objects* (d). *Similar effects influence the apparent size of any distant object, but these effects do not occur in a photograph.*

because we perceive it as being farther away from us than when it is overhead. The images are the same size, but since a faraway object would have to be larger to produce the same size image as a near one, we perceive the object on the horizon as larger. It is the presence of the horizon and the terrain in front of it that tells us that the moon is far away; in the sky overhead there is no such frame of reference. The illusion is enhanced if the moon is seen between buildings or other shapes that provide a frame for it.

The moon illusion is an extreme example of what psychologists call size constancy; the 'correction' of visual images according to what we 'know' the true size of objects to be. Known objects seen at a distance always look larger than the actual size of their images on the retina would indicate.

Here, then, is the reason why 'everything seems so tiny and far away'. The camera does not have the ability to 'correct' images as the mind does, and when we look at the finished picture our minds do not 'correct' it because the element of distance is not present.

In order to make the setting sun appear the same size in a photograph as it does to the eye, it would be necessary to use a longer lens than 'normal' (these terms are explained in Chapter 3) to produce a larger image. This, however, would also make the foreground objects larger and would reduce the angle included in the picture. The only way to make the sun larger while preserving the size of other objects in the picture would be to use a *much* longer lens and take the picture from a great distance. This is exactly what Andreas Feininger and later Emil Schulthess did when they took some of the most widely published pictures of the setting sun and rising moon over New York City. The pictures were made with enormously long lenses from miles away on Long Island or in New Jersey.

It may be helpful to bear in mind that:

Objects at different distances will not have the same relative sizes in a photograph as they have for an observer at the spot from which the photograph is taken.

We have been discussing the example of a sunset chiefly from the standpoint of the image size, because it is the most obvious example of size constancy. In photographing an actual sunset, there are other problems. The range of brightness from the sun itself to the objects in the foreground is usually greater than the film can accommodate. Some of the best sunset pictures are made when the sun itself is hidden by clouds or below the horizon. If the sun is visible and correctly exposed, other objects in the picture will probably be no more than silhouettes.

Emil Schulthess and Emil Spühler used a more elegant arrangement when they made their now-famous panorama of the midnight sun, showing the sun at hourly intervals as it circled in the sky above Arctic Norway. At that latitude in summer the sun dips almost to the horizon but does not set. The two Swiss photographers brought the sun's image within the range of the film by hanging a cardboard disc on threads in front of the camera so that it would block out the sun for part of each exposure. The disc and threads were so far out of focus that they did not register on the film. Incidentally, this set of photographs shows clearly that the sun is the same size at all elevations.

Size constancy always operates, but not always to the same degree. It depends on what we think is the 'true' size of the object. A distant animal will look larger to us if we think it is an elk than if we think it is a deer. There are other attributes of perception that also cannot be reproduced in photography. The human optical system combines an extremely wide angle of view with variable focal length, full-colour stereo vision and a built-in compensating system unequalled by any computer. When a human looks at a scene his eyes dart over it, hesitating for a moment at points of interest, moving backward and forward, up and down. All the various images recorded by the eyes are combined in a visual memory bank into a composite picture somewhat as overlapping aerial photographs are combined into a mosaic in map making. The result is an image that has the characteristics of both long-lens and wide-angle views—a combination that is impossible in a single photograph.

Real landscapes owe some of their impact to the 'wide-screen effect'. They stretch from one edge of the visual field to the other, literally filling the eye. The photograph, on the other hand, is a small flat rectangle surrounded by what is probably a distracting background. Its boundaries are sharply defined; those of the real scene are not. If the photograph were enlarged to cover an entire wall and the observer stood so close to it that it filled his entire visual field, it would look much more like the real thing. This is, of course, precisely what the inventors of the various wide-screen motion-picture systems have been telling us.

The photographer's problem is to create something new within the boundaries of his picture—not a reproduction of the scene, but a selected and organized *part* of it. Often it is only a small part of the scene that makes a good picture. Landscape pictures that try to take in a wide sweep are rarely successful. Similarly, pictures in which *everything* is far away seem flat and uninteresting. One thing we can learn from studies of the moon illusion is that foreground objects help to give a feeling of depth. This fact is not exactly news to artists; they have exploited it for centuries. Its use in photographs is called framing, and it is a standard technique for enhancing the illusion of a third dimension, especially where creating a feeling of depth is a special problem as it is in underwater pictures, fog scenes, and landscapes.

A standard technique is to photograph a landscape from such a position that it will be framed by trees, rocks, or chunks of ice. The objects that make the frame need not be large—low shrubbery or even grass can be used with a low viewpoint. If the framing objects are small, the camera must be relatively close to them and the depth of field must be very great to bring them into focus. A small aperture is indicated, and the camera should be focused at its hyperfocal distance (see Chapter 3). Objects that are at the edge of the picture and serve mainly to lead the eye into the scene do not have to be as sharp as the centre of interest.

Many landscape subjects (with the exception of mountains) are resolutely horizontal in shape and pictures of them tend to show all the subject matter spread out in a thin line across the bottom of a large empty space. I have known photographers to cut branches from a tree and hang them above and in front of the camera like clothes on a line in order to show a fringe of foliage and thus get *something* in the upper part of the picture. If you are fortunate you may have interesting clouds in the sky that can be brought out with a polarizer or an orange filter. This, however, may defeat your purpose by creating a new centre of interest and leading the eye away from the scene. A better solution is to try for a different viewpoint. Raising the camera even a short distance may make it possible to shoot slightly downward and reduce the sky area. It is surprising how much difference a small change in viewpoint can make. Shooting from the roof of a vehicle is some-times enough, and no photographer should be above climbing a tree, if necessary, for his Art.

The weather, season, and time of day play a large part in deter-mining the appearance of a landscape. Dmitri Kessel, a veteran photographer for *Life* magazine, is said to be so experienced at photographing landscapes that he can tell with one glance at a scene the best day and hour to photograph it. The photographer who is able to take his picture at the optimum moment is fortunate indeed, but most of us could do better than we do if we cultivated a sensitivity to the results of changing light and a corresponding ability to imagine its effect on a landscape. Then we might be able to look at a scene and know that at ten o'clock in the morning the light would be at the right angle for a picture. This sort of sensitivity is not really difficult to acquire; people who spend a lot of time out of doors become accustomed to the different angles of the sun even without being aware of them. This is one factor in the mysterious sense of direction that outdoorsmen and Indians are reputed to possess. It has been proven conclusively that these people do not have any better senses than the rest of us; they are just more observant, consciously or unconsciously.

Landscapes differ so much that there is no general rule for choosing the best time to photograph one, but the middle of the day is usually the worst time. With the sun high in the sky, texture, modelling, and depth are reduced and colours washed out. The early morning is apt to be the best time, and the late afternoon next. The reddish colour of sunlight at those times can easily be corrected with a 'cooling' (bluish) filter. Early morning light with the proper filter will make colours appear brighter, clearer, and with more contrast than will the traditional midday sun. Early rising may make a landscape photographer healthy and wise, as well as improving his pictures. There is, however, no danger of his becoming wealthy!

The Human Interest Question

For years photographers have been advised to include a person in every landscape picture to give it 'human interest' and provide 'scale'. The theory is that people are more interested in other people than they are in landscapes, and that by including a person in the picture we can trick them into looking at the scenery. This always reminds me of a television commercial for dog food in which the announcer is a dog. No doubt he provides canine interest.

I am not quite sure, but I suspect that I am more interested in landscapes than I am in people. At any rate, I have seen so many landscapes with people standing in the foreground looking into the distance that I am bored with them. For me, one of the most attractive features of mountain scenes is that they are *not* inhabited by people.

Foreground figures have a reason for being there if the purpose of the picture is to show Aunt Minnie at the Grand Canyon. Such a picture is a perfectly valid snapshot. But foreground figures that do not have a reason for being there should not be included. They are a cliché and a cheap substitute for good composition.

It is true that putting a person in the foreground will give a feeling of depth to a picture and make distant objects look more natural. However, this occurs because they are in the foreground and not because they are people. Natural objects that belong there will do the same job better. Using a person does not give us any scale of comparison by which to judge something like the height of a mountain.

If we are truly interested in nature photography, we should be willing to let nature speak for itself.

Plants

There are a few special problems in photographing plants that deserve mention. Flowers are probably the most photographed plants, and they may also be among the most frustrating plants to photograph, especially in colour.

The colours of some flowers are actually quite complex, with a distribution of wavelengths that cannot be duplicated on film. As we mentioned in Chapter 5, colours that look the same may be produced in different ways. They may, as a result, react differently to changes in illumination. They may also photograph differently. The colour we see when we look at a colour picture is not derived from the original subject; it is produced by dyes that are added to the film in processing. Mixtures of these dye colours can approximate most flower colours, but not all. There is also another possible source of error: the way the colour is *recorded* by the film may not match its appearance to the eye.

For example, the colour violet in a rainbow is produced by short wavelengths of light. But certain flowers that appear violet or lavender to the eye will usually come out pink in a photograph. Among these are the heavenly blue morning glory and the lavender ageratum. When scientists at Eastman Kodak subjected the light reflected by these flowers to spectrographic analysis it was found that their colour is composed of two bands of wavelengths, one in the blue region and the other, which is the more intense of the two, at the extreme of the red region. The human eye has little sensitivity to the extreme red wavelengths, so the flowers appear predominantly blue to us. But to a colour film, the red wavelengths are stronger than the blue ones and so the flowers photograph pink.

Once its cause has been determined, the discrepancy between eye sensitivity and film sensitivity can be approximately corrected by the right combination of filters. In this case a Wratten No. 66 (a light green, ordinarily used to increase contrast with red-stained specimens in microscopy) and two CC-50M (magenta) filters are used with daylight-type film under studio incandescent illumination at 3200° K. If daylight illumination is used, a Wratten No. 85B (orange) filter must be added to the pack. The exposure increase required by the filters is 5 stops for the incandescent light and $5\frac{2}{3}$ stops for daylight.

Finding the right filters for colours as complicated as these requires equipment that few photographers would have available. Fortunately, this is an extreme case. For most flower colours the corrections, if any are needed, can be found visually. But for really accurate colour it is necessary to shoot tests and have them processed for evaluation before the final photographs are made. Some flowers do not stay in bloom long enough to permit such tests. For them, only experience and luck will serve.

When tests can be made, they should be made on film of the same manufacturing batch as that to be used for the final picture. The particular batch is indicated by an emulsion number stamped on the package. Since all the packages in each case received by a dealer ordinarily come from the same batch, it is not too difficult to get a uniform supply of film if it is all bought at one time. Tests should be made in a series, with exposures varying by $\frac{1}{2}$ stop from 2 stops over the exposure indicated by the meter to 2 stops under it. If the exposure requires correction for bellows extension or magnification (see Chapter 8) the corrected exposure should, of course, be taken as the midpoint of the series. It may be helpful to include in a corner of the picture a small tag identifying the exposure as 'normal', '$\frac{1}{2}$ stop over', '$\frac{1}{2}$ stop under', and so on. The exposure that produces the best colour rendering is the one to use.

If the colour does not match the visual effect of the flower, a correction can be estimated as follows. View the transparency on a light box of standard colour (such as those made by photographic manufactuers). Try placing colour-correction filters over the transparency until one or more are found that give the flower a natural-looking colour. The filter to use in taking the final picture will then be the same colour *but one half the density* of the filter that gives the best correction over the transparency. A filter used over the lens when the exposure is made has approximately twice the effect of one used over the finished transparency. If, for example, a CC-20Y gives the best colour rendering when placed over the transparency, then a CC-10Y should be used to make the picture. One can only hope that the colour correction necessary for the flower will not give unsatisfactory rendering of other colours in the picture.

It is possible, incidentally, to correct the colour balance in a transparency *within limits* after the transparency is made and processed. When transparencies are used to make plates for printing, colour corrections are almost always made (and so are corrections in contrast and density). Similar corrections are possible if the transparency is used to make a positive print or duplicate transparency, but only those of the more expensive laboratory class, since the inexpensive mass-production printing and duplicating services are not equipped to make corrections. It is not so well known that original transparencies can, as a last resort, be sandwiched together with pieces of tinted film to alter the overall colour balance. These films are available in sheets, in a great variety of colours, from art-supply stores.

Flowers in Black-and-White

We have been talking, so far, about the problems of photographing flowers in colour. There is a different set of problems when flowers are photographed in black-and-white. Colours that look quite different in nature or in a colour photograph may come out the same shade of grey when translated into black-and-white. It is comparatively easy to control colour rendering in black-and-white with filters; the problem is that it must be done 'blind'. There is no way the photographer can see in advance the grey tones that will be produced by the various colours. He can, however, learn to predict them.

Movie directors of hand-cranked camera days used to look through a blue filter to see how the scene would look on film. The early stock was sensitive only to blue, but blue-sensitive (or 'colour-blind') film has now been relegated to technical applications and panchromatic ('all-colour') film has supplanted it. Although panchromatic film does record all the colours we see, it does not record them with the same relative intensities that we see. It is more sensitive to blue than is the eye, and less sensitive to yellow. Thus blue flowers (and blue skies) are rendered too light, while yellow flowers appear too dark. If a white flower is photographed against a blue sky, both the sky and the flower may be white in the photograph. Similarly, a yellow flower against a background of green leaves may disappear, because the yellow and the green are both translated into the same shade of grey.

The medium yellow filter is the most useful one, by far, for correcting the sensitivity of panchromatic films. It lightens yellows and darkens blues so that in most situations it renders colours with about the intensity that they have when we see them. It is impossible to be precise, of course, when comparing vision in full colour with photography in monochrome.

But the brightnesses that we see are not necessarily enough to separate a flower from its background in a photograph. When we look at the flower we not only see it in full colour, we also see it with two eyes. It will stand out from its background much more in nature than in any photograph, and much more in a colour photograph than a black-and-white one. To show the subject adequately against its background it may be necessary to depart from the brightnesses that an observer would see. Since the photographer cannot see his results in advance, he must experiment and rely on experience. A filter will render objects of its own colour lighter and those of a complementary colour darker. Intermediate colours may be lighter or darker depending on the characteristics of the filter—characteristics that cannot be distinguished by looking at it. To a certain extent, however, the effect can be judged by looking at the subject through the filter. On a

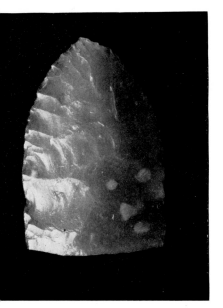

[15] *How to photograph an arrowhead (see page 108). Unsatisfactory approaches include: diffused lighting (top left); direct side lighting (top right); and side lighting with black background (bottom left). Best arrangement has arrowhead on glass, background lighted separately (bottom right).*

[16] *Spiny lobsters seek protection of a poisonous, long-spined se urchin. Photographed with a 'look box' from the surface (see page 140).*

camera that has ground-glass viewing, a better estimate can be made by putting the filter on the camera and examining the image.

A green filter is useful for black-and-white photography of plants because it makes foliage lighter and the sky darker. An orange filter is similar in effect to a yellow one, but the effect is increased. Each colour is available in two or three degrees of density. Naturally, they require an increase in exposure because only part of the light is permitted to reach the film. There are exposure tables for the more common filters on the instruction sheets packed with some rolls of film. They are also printed in handbooks and pocket guides.

It is often helpful to modify the background when photographing a flower. Some flowers can best be photographed from a low angle so that the sky will form the background. If there is any blue colour in the sky it can be rendered darker with filters. In other cases it is a good idea to throw a shadow behind the flower to keep the background from being too distracting. Some photographers carry sheets of cardboard that either can be used to throw a shadow or can be placed behind the flower (far enough behind to be out of focus) to make an artificial background.

Motion

The other special problem of photographing plants arises from their movement. It is the nature of plants to be almost constantly in motion. We think of an oak tree as a symbol of stability, yet if you sit and watch one for a while on any but the stillest of days you will see the branches nodding and the leaves quivering.

In a photograph of an entire tree, which must necessarily be taken from some distance to get the whole tree in, it is possible to stop the movement with a shutter speed of 1/250 or even 1/100 sec. A close-up of a flower, leaf, or seed is another matter. The smaller the subject of a photograph is, the harder it is to stop its motion. This is because the motion with which we are concerned— that which makes the picture look unsharp—is not really the motion of the subject but the motion of the *image* on the film. If the camera is 100 feet away from a tree, the distance that the image of a single leaf will move in 1/100 sec., may be 1/1000 in., which is not enough to be noticeable in the final print. If the camera is one foot away from the same leaf, the same amount of movement will cause the image to move 1/10 in. and the picture will be blurred.

No camera shutter is fast enough to stop motion in an extreme close-up. Electronic flash units can do it, but it is generally not practical to use them in a situation like our example, for two reasons. First, the small, battery-operated portable units are not very fast—1/500 to 1/1500 sec.—and the units that deliver high speeds are heavy and require electric power lines. Second, unless the electronic flash is used in near darkness, there will be time while the shutter is open for some of the other light to register before and after the flash. If the subject is moving, this will result in 'ghost' images—a vague blur around or in addition to the sharp image.

If the subject is very small, the motion problem is complicated by the necessity of allowing extra exposure to compensate for the magnification (see Chapter 8) and also to permit use of the very small apertures necessary for adequate depth of field.

Electronic flash is more helpful for tiny subjects than for larger ones because if the light only has to cover a small area it can be very close to the subject, and in that case the aperture can be so small that no other light will register and ghost images will not occur. For tiny subjects electronic flash tubes are available in 'ring light' form—a doughnut-shaped flash tube that fits around the lens and helps to solve the twin problems of how to get the light in the right place and how to get the shadows (caused by the light) behind the subject where they don't show. The trouble is that these lights won't light up the background, so the picture is likely to look like a night scene.

It is generally better to try to minimize the motion and then wait for an instant when the subject is still. If it is a leaf or flower that grows on a branch, the branch can be tied down or propped up to hold it steady. If it is a flower near the ground, the photographer can use his rucksack as a windbreak on one side and his body on another. He may want to rig up a portable windbreak of cloth with a long, thin metal rod in a hem at each end that can be stuck into the ground to hold it in place. An improved version of this venerable device can be made from transparent plastic sheeting. It will cut off the wind but not the light.

If you watch a blowing flower carefully you will see that its movement has a pattern, and that somewhere in that pattern there is a moment of rest. This is true because the flower is attached to a stem that has a certain degree of flexibility and is fastened down where it enters the earth. The flower is like a pendulum, but its motion is much more complicated. Somewhere there is a neutral position, and the flower will pause there before starting a new gyration. It has been suggested that the pause always occurs just before the photographer has set up his equipment, but actually it is bound to recur periodically. The problem is to anticipate it. Photographers vary in the length of time it takes them to trip the shutter after they have decided to do so, but reaction times as long as 1/5 sec. are not unusual. This is longer than a flower is likely to stay still, so the photographer must learn to start the process just *before* the subject comes to rest. With practice, a high degree of skill can be acquired, but there will always be times when the subject does not come to rest when you think it is going to, or the timing fails. Often it is impossible to be sure until the film is processed whether the subject was caught at the right moment. Therefore a number of exposures should always be made. An ample supply of film should always be carried when photographing flowers in the field.

The technique of studying the subject's characteristic motion, finding the moment of rest, and then trying to anticipate it, is not limited to flowers. It is discussed in relation to other subjects in Chapter 13.

8:

Photographing Small Objects

A SURPRISINGLY large proportion of nature photography involves objects small enough to require special photographic techniques. Whether the subjects be fossils, birds' eggs, meteorites, ice crystals, or flowers, the problems of close-up photography are the same.

Standard photographic techniques and equipment are designed for photographing objects the size of a man and larger. Smaller objects must usually be photographed from a closer viewpoint. Ordinary methods of measuring light and computing exposure are actually correct only when the camera is focused at infinity, but the error is negligible for working distances down to eight or ten times the focal length of the lens.

The light-gathering power of a lens, as we saw in Chapter 3, is determined by the diameter of the lens opening in relation to the focal length. This is what f-numbers measure. But for greatest precision we should use not the focal length but the lens-to-film distance. These two distances are identical when the lens is focused at infinity, and at normal working distances they are similar enough that no error results from the convenience of using the focal length (which is constant) instead of the lens-to-film distance (which changes with every change in focus).

At short working distances, the lens-to-film distance increases rapidly and the focal length can no longer be used to approximate it. Because the lens-to-film distance is the bottom half of the fraction that represents light-gathering power, that quantity becomes smaller as the lens-to-film distance increases and in close-ups the effective aperture, or light-gathering power, is materially smaller than that indicated on the aperture scale.

Another way of expressing this is to say that the same amount of light is gathered by the lens as at normal distances, but it is spread over a much larger total image, of which only part is being used. The intensity of light at any one point is therefore less than it would be if the entire image were not magnified. Consequently the exposure must be increased to compensate for the magnification.

This is one reason why simple cameras often do not focus closer than 3 feet. Such cameras, if they use roll film in the popular 120 or 620 size, usually have lenses with focal lengths of 75 to 85 mm. (3 to 3½ inches). The 3-foot limit is roughly equal to 10 times this focal length, and is the nearest point at which normal exposures can be used without correction.

At a distance of 3 feet, an 80-mm. lens on a 120 reflex camera will photograph a field about 2 feet square. To fill the frame with an object smaller than that, the camera must be moved closer to the subject. This involves three families of problems, which we will consider in turn. The three families are focus, exposure, and lighting.

Focus

To focus on an object closer than the normal limit of the camera, we must either move the lens farther away from the film or change the focal length of the lens. For simple cameras with non-interchangeable lenses only the second choice is possible. It is done with extra elements called 'close-up attachments', which fit over the regular lens as eyeglasses fit over the eye. These attachments are inexpensive and quite satisfactory. They do not require any adjustment in exposure because, by adding another lens element, they reduce the focal length of the lens. The lens-to-film distance is not increased beyond that used at normal distances. Such attachments work only within a limited range of distances, but several different ones can be interchanged or used in combination to achieve various magnifications. For twin-lens reflex cameras and for some range-finder cameras there are also attachments that 'correct' the image in the viewfinder so that it will show approximately what area is covered when the auxiliary lens is used. Even with these correcting devices, it is difficult to see just what the camera is getting and where the zone of sharp focus lies. That is the chief disadvantage of close-up attachments. Also, the image they produce is not always as sharp as that of a lens operating at the focal length for which it was designed.

A better way of obtaining a large image of a small object is to move the lens farther away from the film (and closer to the subject). This is easy to do with a view camera or press camera, especially if it has extra track and bellows. These cameras have ground-glass screens for focusing (thereby solving the problem of how to see what the camera sees), and are unquestionably the best choice for close-up photography of objects that do not move. They are heavy and difficult to set up, however, and may not be a good choice for work in the field or with live subjects.

Smaller cameras, particularly 35-mm. ones, are more manoeuvrable. If the lens can be removed, it can be set farther from the film by using extension rings, tubes, or bellows interposed between the lens and the camera body. Among small cameras, the single-lens reflex is the most convenient type for close-ups because viewing and focusing are done through the lens that takes the picture. Several possible sources of error are thus eliminated. Before the recent wave of popularity of single-lens reflex cameras, 'copying outfits' were used with many standard range-finder cameras. These accessories use a small ground-glass screen in place of the camera for viewing and focusing. Just before the exposure, the camera must be substituted for the viewing screen. This is a clumsy arrangement. The single-lens reflex accomplishes the same result with an almost instantaneous flip of the mirror, and is much more satisfactory.

On any camera that has a removable lens, considerable magnification can be obtained by using a shorter-than-normal lens, even one designed for a smaller camera. The image of a mosquito will fill a 5 × 7-inch negative if a 2-inch movie camera lens is used in place of the normal 9-inch lens. At ordinary working distances such a short lens would not 'cover' the film (that is, the flat field in which a sharp image is formed would not be large enough), but in extreme close-ups the field is magnified, just as the subject is.

When the size of the image is to exceed the size of the subject, many lenses should be mounted backward. This is because most lenses are designed to form an image of an object that is comparatively far away, and project that image on to a plane (the film) that is relatively close. Most lenses, therefore, are designed to have differing optical characteristics in 'front' and 'back'. The front should face toward the longer of the two distances. Thus, if the film is farther from the lens than the subject is, the lens may give a better image if it is reversed so that its front faces the film. Test photographs should be made to see if the image formed by a particular lens is improved by reversing it. Various bushings and threaded rings are available to hold lenses in the reversed position, or one can be made by any well-equipped camera repair shop. Unfortunately, only a few of the commercial close-up attachments provide for reversing the lens. Even fewer manufacturers provide any means for attaching a lens shade to the back of the lens when it is used in reverse, although the 'press-on' type of adaptor rings will work on some lenses. Shading the lens is just as important in close-up work as in any other kind of photography, and the photographer must devise a way to hold a shade in place, even if it is only a strip of masking tape.

Exceptions to the reversing rule are lenses designed specifically for close work, such as copying or engraving, and lenses of symmetrical design, with front and back optically identical. Enlarging lenses are designed for short-range work, but even so, most of them should be mounted backward. Since enlarging lenses do not have shutters, they may prove inconvenient on cameras where the exposure is ordinarily controlled by a shutter in the lens. In the absence of either a focal plane or between-the-lens shutter, long exposures can always be controlled by turning the lights on and off or by removing and replacing a lens cap. The latter method was good enough for Mathew Brady, but most photographers today consider it imprecise.

Modern 35-mm. single-lens reflex cameras have internally coupled automatic diaphragms. There is a button or lever inside the lens mount (usually mounted on the film side) that closes the diaphragm to a predetermined stop. This button or lever is ordinarily actuated by a cam in the camera body when the photographer presses the shutter release. When such lenses are mounted on extension tubes or bellows to place them farther from the film, or when they are reversed, the diaphragm is no longer automatic and must be stopped down manually just before the exposure.

There are some lenses specially designed for close-up work that have double-extension lens mounts, permitting them to focus as close as one-to-one (the image is the same size as the subject) without accessories. At least one such lens, the Micro-Nikkor, has a diaphragm that functions automatically even when the lens is extended, and is arranged to compensate for the necessary increase in exposure by giving a wider aperture as the magnification increases. Some others are calibrated to indicate the necessary increase in exposure. Opening the lens diaphragm is not the best way of increasing the exposure, however, because a small aperture is usually necessary to get satisfactory depth of field.

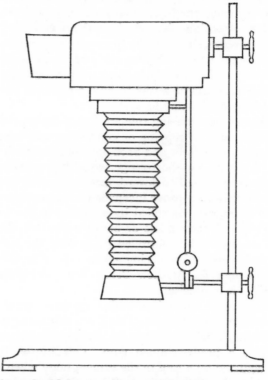

Fig. 20 A standard laboratory ring stand is a convenient camera support for close-up photography. A rigid stand is necessary because any vibration is magnified.

At short distances and great magnifications, any camera movement will be magnified. It is thus essential that the camera be firmly mounted on a tripod or clamp. Two tripods—one under the camera body and the other under the lens—are even better. No camera support has yet been invented that is really satisfactory for close-up work in the field, but for work in the lab or studio the standard laboratory ring stand and its many attachments are very convenient.

In any close-up where the size of the image approaches the size of the subject, the best focusing procedure is to leave the camera and lens stationary and move *the subject* into focus. If a precise degree of magnification is required (as where different subjects are to be compared and must be to the same scale) the lens-to-film distance should be found from a published table and the lens should be locked at that distance. The subject should then be brought into focus by changing only the lens-to-subject distance. Otherwise, it may be impossible to find any point of sharp focus if the lens is moved back and forth in the usual way. This is because moving the lens closer to the film simultaneously moves it farther from the subject. The effect is negligible at normal distances, but may completely defeat the attempt to focus on a close subject.

It may be convenient to remember that the total distance from film to subject cannot be less than four times the focal length of the lens. The lens may move forward or back within that distance, but as it gets closer to the subject it must be farther from the film. If the sum of the lens-to-film distance and the lens-to-subject distance is less than four times the focal length, no point of sharp focus can be found.

Many natural subjects, of course, cannot be moved to bring them into focus, so the next best method is to move the camera and lens as a unit. Extension bellows of 'double track' design are to be preferred over 'single track' models because they have tripod connections on the track that allow the camera and lens to be moved either independently or together.

Depth of field (the distance between the nearest and farthest points that are in sharp focus) is extremely shallow in close-ups. The lens diaphragm must usually be stopped down to a very small aperture to bring all of the subject into focus. Frequently the smallest aperture available on the lens is insufficient to bring all of the subject into focus. This is a most distressing discovery to make when it is made afterward, as it often is when there is not enough light for the photographer to see the depth of field clearly before he takes the picture. He should remember, however, that the minimum apertures on most lenses are there for a reason: If the lens were stopped down farther the resolution would not be adequate. Lenses that are specially designed for close-up work usually stop down farther than ordinary lenses, but their *maximum* apertures are not as large.

There is one way—and only one—of getting greater depth of field when the lens is stopped down as far as it will go. That way is to reduce the size of the image. Use only part of the negative, if necessary, and enlarge it more in printing. Changing to a sharper, finer-grained (and probably slower) film may make this feasible.

The use of a small aperture to get depth of field requires either a very long exposure or a lot of light, or both, and it compounds the already acute problem of close-up exposure.

Exposure

The exposure that is indicated by an exposure meter is, as mentioned above, applicable only at normal distances (i.e., more than ten times the focal length of the lens). At shorter distances the indicated exposure must be multiplied by a factor that increases very rapidly as magnification is increased. This factor is usually called the 'bellows extension factor' although it really results from the magnification and not from the extension of the bellows. The magnification involved is in the size of the image on the film, as compared with the subject itself. Further magnification may be introduced later in enlarging, but it does not affect the exposure factor. When the image produced on the negative is the same size as the subject, the exposure indicated by a meter must be quadrupled. For an image twice as big as the subject, the exposure factor is 9!

There are several formulas for computing factors for other magnifications. They involve the lens-to-film distance and the focal length of the lens, but it is not necessary to use them. All that really matters is the size of the image in relation to the size of the subject. A few years ago, some genius at Eastman Kodak devised a little ruler that gives exposure factors directly for any camera with ground-glass viewing. A target 2 inches across is temporarily placed next to the subject, the image of this 2-inch target on the ground glass is measured with the ruler, and the answer is read directly in exposure factors. This ruler is included in the Kodak Master Photoguide.

On 35-mm. cameras, the ground glass (if there is one) is too small to be used for making measurements. But a similar ruler can be used at the subject to find exposure factors for various sizes of the field. Such a ruler is reproduced for use with this book. If, for example, the area included in the picture measures $3\frac{1}{2}$ inches long at the subject, the exposure factor is 2, and the exposure indicated by a meter should be doubled.

For greater magnification or for cameras that are not 35-mm. size and have no ground glass, a little cardboard 'Effective Aperture Computer' is available. It is a specialized, circular slide rule. As a last resort, the formula

$$A_e = \frac{A_i \times V}{F}$$

in which A_e is the effective aperture, A_i is the indicated aperture, V is the lens-to-film distance and F, the focal length, can be computed on paper.

Lighting

Effective lighting must reveal the significant features of the subject without looking unnatural. Also, of course, it must provide enough illumination to expose the film properly. A third function, in close-up work, is to enable the photographer to see what his camera is getting and when the image is in focus. These requirements, which are given in order of importance, sometimes conflict. The photographer who works out of doors and uses only sunlight is not any less responsible for the lighting in his pictures than the photographer who stays home and uses floodlights. In no case should the lighting call attention to itself.

Photographers who specialize in wildlife consider it unsporting to photograph animals that have been tamed or confined in any way. They do not seem to mind, however, if the light in their pictures comes from such an angle that it could not possibly be natural. In nature, light usually comes from above, but seldom from directly overhead. About half the time the dominant light source is *behind* the subject. There is usually light of lesser intensity coming from other directions, but *never* are there two light sources of equal intensity. The same natural pattern should be followed in lighting a photographic subject. Film does not have as great a range of sensitivity as the eye, however, so shadows in the scene should not be as dark or highlights as bright, comparatively, as they would be in nature.

The lighting of close-ups is by far the most difficult part of this sort of photography. Since each subject presents individual problems, great patience and ingenuity are required. A light or reflector is moved slightly and the result studied. Then the light is moved a little more; there is no other way. There are, however, a few tips that may reduce the time spent in arranging the lights.

Subjects with surface texture should be lighted from an angle so that the texture will be revealed by shadows; translucent subjects should be lighted at least partly from behind. Shadows should never be allowed to interfere with the natural contours of an object, and each object should be separated from others nearby and from the background. A subject with a glossy surface should ordinarily show a few reflections to indicate its character, but surface reflections should never obscure the colour and shading underneath. One universal rule of thumb is that the more light sources there are, the more problems will be created.

Any light source can be used for close-ups. In the field, excellent work can be done with sunlight alone if reflectors, mirrors, and even small lenses are used to control it. Flash and electronic flash are also used, but they require extra care because the photographer cannot see and judge their effect before he takes the picture. The usual guide numbers used for determining exposures with flash will not work for close-ups because the bulb and reflector do not act as a point source of light when they are very close to the subject. Special reduced guide numbers must be derived by actual test.

With subjects that move, however, flash and electronic flash have the advantages of stopping motion and of not producing very much heat. For subjects that do not move, these devices present the possibility of building up an enormous amount of light by repeating the flash as many times as necessary.

Let us try to apply the precepts above to an actual situation—a picture of an arrowhead 1 inch long (see Plate 15). Since our purpose is to make a scientific record, we will photograph it 'squarely'— with the film parallel to the chief plane of the subject—so that no part of the object is rendered larger or smaller by perspective.

Therefore, we put the arrowhead on a piece of white paper on a table and set the camera, pointing straight down, directly over it. Now we can start lighting.

First we look through the viewer and centre the arrowhead in the frame. It looks pretty good, so we decide that perhaps diffused lighting will be best. The ordinary room lighting isn't quite right, however, so we decide to build a 'tent'. This is an enclosure, usually of white paper, that surrounds the subject and reflects light from all sides. We wrap a piece of paper into a cone with the lens aimed—through a hole in the apex—at the arrowhead in the centre of the base. There isn't room to put any lights inside, so we shine a floodlight through the paper from the outside.

The arrowhead stands out nicely, but now we find that the texture of the surface has disappeared!

Folding our tent, we silently go back to direct lighting. We shine a floodlight from one side, and find that at a low angle the texture is brought out in stark relief. The side away from the light, however, is hidden in shadow. We bring up another light on the dark side and get it lighted up, too. But now we see distracting shadows on the background. We move the lights around, trying to discover a position that will eliminate the shadows without eliminating the surface texture. If we can only put the shadows where they will be hidden by the subject itself, the shadow problem will be solved. Finally, we discover that as we move the lights close to the lens the shadows get smaller. In order to eliminate them completely, though, the light and the lens would have to be at the same spot. This is not quite as impossible as it sounds, because doughnut-shaped light sources do exist. Electronic flash tubes are made in circular form, with provision for the lens to look through the centre of the ring. Fluorescent tubes are also made in circles, and a reasonably ingenious photographer can make a reflector for one from a cake tin.

A more common solution is to use a reflector of white paper, cloth, or metal foil and bounce the light from it on to the subject. The lens can be stuck through a hole in the reflector. Of course, the lens must be shaded from direct light to avoid reflections inside the lens that might interefere with the image.

If we use a light at the camera axis to photograph our arrowhead, we will find that the shadows have been conquered, but that the texture is gone, too, and the whole picture looks dull. Very well.

Let us go back to the two-light set-up. We can improve it some-what by using a reflector (a sheet of white cardboard) in place of the second light. This softens some of the shadows and auto-matically makes the light on one side of the subject dominant—a situation that generally looks more natural than evenly balanced lighting. The shadow cast by the main light is still disturbing, however, and at this point there is usually a temptation to try to drown the shadows by making the background black. If we try it, we will find that the black background makes the subject look too light, the texture becomes less apparent, and the shadows are still visible, anyway.

The next move is to put the arrowhead on a sheet of glass and put the background under it, far enough below so that the shadows will be outside the picture. To make sure that they are outside, we temporarily focus the camera on the background and check. Then, focusing again on the subject, we note with satisfaction that the texture is brought out nicely and the shadows have been eliminated. However, the quality of the material doesn't quite emerge. The flint is actually translucent near the edges where it was chipped very thin, and it has a hard, shiny surface.

To emphasize those qualities we make two more changes in the lighting. First, we fasten a small mirror from a lady's handbag just outside the picture so that it reflects a beam of light across the highest part of the arrowhead, causing a few bright highlights that perk up the surface and show how hard and shiny it is. Then we take away the paper background and replace it with a sheet of opal glass (or plain glass covered with tracing paper). We put another light behind the background and find that by moving it closer or farther away we can make the background lighter or darker and can bring out a bit of the translucent quality of the flint.

Now we are ready to take the picture. We measure the size of the field included in our frame and determine the exposure factor. We turn off the background light while we take a meter reading, to avoid misleading the meter with light from the background. Then we stop down the lens aperture and examine the image carefully. It is so faint that it is hard to see anything, but our eyes adapt, and finally we see a bright silver streak across the middle of the picture. We look at the subject again—no streak. Then, at last, we see it. It is a reflection of the front of the camera in the glass on which the subject rests. We didn't see it before because it was out of focus until the lens was stopped down. We get a piece of black paper, cut a hole in the centre, and slip it over the lens.

When we finally open the shutter (using a cable release to avoid jarring the camera) it seems like an anticlimax, but that is the way good close-ups are made.

9:

Photography in the Field

AS the urban megaloctopus creeps across the land, spawning split-level suburbs between its super-highway tentacles, the nature photographer has to go farther and farther afield to find any nature. Algae, of course, can be collected in a city park, but larger forms of wildlife must usually be sought in the wilds. Journeying beyond the highways and power lines not only restoreth the soul, it also provides a good antidote for the exaggerated belief in great quantities of equipment, which is chronic among photography fans and even infects some working professionals.

The Backpacker's Philosophy

In the far woods, deserts, and mountains, he who carries the least can go the farthest and may come back with the most and best pictures. Carrying everything on one's back develops an attitude that is at once ascetic and practical. 'Backpackers' ask not 'What can I take?' but 'What can I leave out?' They disdain any item that can be used for only one purpose, and anything that remains unused by the end of a trip will be left behind the next time. Their simple but effective discipline could serve as an example to most photographers.

Many of the best natural subjects are in places accessible only on foot, on horseback, by dog-sled, or canoe. To photograph them successfully, equipment must be rigorously selected for maximum utility combined with minimum weight and bulk. The Appalachian Trail Conference, which ought to know, suggests a maximum load for extended hiking of 35 pounds for a man or 30 pounds for a woman. Pay load for a burro is 100 pounds; for a canoe, about

[17] *Greater Black-Backed Gull following a ship in the Outer Hebrides.*

[18] *Demoiselle Crane, Anthropoides virgo, photographed in the New York Zoo. A large aperture was used to throw the background out of focus (see page 157).*

200 pounds in addition to the paddlers (but canoe loads become hiking loads when a portage is reached).

Minimum personal equipment for a weekend—sleeping bag, clothing, food, and cooking utensils and a pack in which to carry them—will weigh about 20 pounds per person if wisely chosen; more if the traveller is inexperienced. An ordinary gadget bag with two small cameras, several lenses, film, filters, accessories, and small flash unit weighs about 20 pounds. If the photographer wants to arrive sufficiently fresh to take pictures, he would be wise to keep his load well below the maximum, so simple arithmetic indicates that something will have to be eliminated if he is to make more than one-day trips.

Reducing the equipment load is not only possible, it is good discipline. It teaches one to use his head instead of his back. At home one may use one camera for colour and another for black-and-white; in the field a single camera must serve, with film being changed as needed.

Better yet, the photographer might standardize on colour negative film, from which he can later get colour transparencies, colour prints, black-and-white prints, or printing plates at will. This new material is as fast as a medium-speed black-and-white film and offers the greatest flexibility possible on one film. It can be used to make colour pictures under any illumination (thus eliminating the several different types of film that would otherwise be required) because the correction for the colour of the light is made later in printing instead of at the time of exposure. The adaptability of colour negative film for field use is a good reason for nature photographers to become familiar with it.

Cameras

A camera for mobile field photography should be sturdy, adaptable, compact, and light. The necessary accessories and film supply must also meet these requirements. This eliminates all cameras that use sheet film because they require not only film holders (an adequate number of which may weigh as much as the camera) but also a changing bag in which the holders can be reloaded.

On all counts, the 35-mm. camera is the best choice for this type of work. It will make 576 exposures on a pound of film, and is the lightest practical type. (The sub-miniatures that use film less than 35-mm. wide are not yet well-enough developed to offer any competition.) Among 35-mm. cameras, the older and simpler models are better for field use than many new ones.

As cameras have become more 'modern' they have become heavier. Much of the added weight contributes nothing to the effectiveness of the mechanism, and it is hard to escape the suspicion that some of it is there simply to make the customer feel he is getting something for all that money.

Cameras with bellows are not as sturdy as those with solid lens mountings, and are not a good choice because their lenses are not interchangeable.

If much of the photography is to be close-up or long-lens work, a single-lens reflex camera would be best. The range-finder camera, however, is lighter and is better for medium distances. In either case, extension tubes should be carried if any close-ups are planned. The tubes are more satisfactory than either auxiliary lenses or extension bellows.

Many of the older range-finder 35-mm. cameras had lenses which, with a quarter-turn to unlock them, could be collapsed into the body of the camera. These collapsible-mount lenses are relatively slow ($f/3.5$ to $f/2$) but many of them are of excellent quality, and larger apertures are rarely used in the field. Since many such lenses are now out of production and out of fashion, the prices of used ones are low.

Cameras of older vintage *may* be good choices if they have not had too much wear. They are likely to be lighter and more compact than current models. An exception to this rule is the single-lens reflex, which did not really come into its own until the late 1950s.

It is worth considering the purchase of a special camera—simple, sturdy, and light—exclusively for field work. Alternatively, one could use the same camera body for everything, but with a lighter, collapsible-mount lens for use in the field. With this lens attached, the camera would fit a smaller case.

There are even a few long-focus lenses with collapsible mounts. They sometimes turn up in second-hand camera stores. Lenses do not wear out (although they can be damaged) and old ones may be perfectly good. They must be adjusted to focus properly on the camera on which they will be used. The camera repair technician who does the adjusting would be likely to uncover any serious deficiency in the lens at the same time. The checking and adjusting should be done during the guarantee or free trial period so that the lens can be returned for a full refund if it is not satisfactory. No photographic equipment should be purchased without such a guarantee.

Lenses

For photographing wildlife, long lenses are usually required. They are unavoidably heavy, because optical glass is dense and quite a lot of it is used in long lenses. Slower lenses (those whose maximum aperture is smaller) are smaller, lighter, and less expensive than fast lenses of the same focal length. They are quite satisfactory for work in good light. Lenses with barrels made of aluminium alloys instead of nickel-plated brass are materially lighter. They are hard to keep steady when hand held, but are satisfactory at high shutter speeds or when the camera is used on a firm support. There are also a few 'convertible' long-focus lenses which come apart so that the pieces can be used singly or in combination to yield two or three different focal lengths from one lens (see Plate 22). All of them are slow.

Some saving of weight and a great increase in convenience are provided by the new 'zoom' or variable focal-length lenses for single-lens reflex cameras. The best ones have automatic diaphragms, stay focused on the same spot when the focal length is changed, and are comparable in quality to fixed focal-length lenses. Although zoom lenses are long and heavy, they are lighter than the four or five individual lenses that might otherwise be needed to cover the same range of focal lengths, and they are easier to use. The photographer who is on top of a mountain peak cannot move in for a closer view or back for a wider one; he must either change lenses or change the focal length of a variable lens.

Artificial Light and Daylight

Artificial light sources are ordinarily ruled out for field work because of their weight, but some special situations may require them. For photographing nocturnal subjects or cave interiors, miniature flash bulbs give the most light per ounce. It should be remembered that a single artificial light source rarely produces satisfying pictures, so equipment should be available to introduce back and side light as well as front light.

Where high speeds are needed to stop motion, electronic flash is the only answer. Strobe (electronic flash) units have been greatly improved in recent years, and there are now battery-powered units that are truly portable and give a great deal of light. Some of the increased light output has been obtained by lengthening the flash duration, which reduces its ability to stop motion. Therefore a unit should be tested to ensure that its speed is fast enough for the intended use *before* it is taken into the field. Another point that should be checked is the number of flashes that can be expected from one set of batteries. If spare batteries are required, their weight must be added to that of the unit in comparing it with others. Manufacturers' claims regarding battery life should be verified by test.

For producing enormous quantities of light nothing can surpass old-fashioned flash powder. It is still being made, although suppliers who stock it may be hard to find. It must be handled with great care because of the danger of explosion, and it should not be used in confined spaces because it produces enough smoke to make a second exposure impossible. Flash powder does not synchronize with the camera shutter as electrical flashes do, but the blast can be delayed by means of a fuse like those used with dynamite to give the photographer time to get back to the camera and open the shutter.

If a continuous light source (rather than a flash) is required, there are still ways of providing one far from electric power lines. Petrol pressure lanterns or vehicle headlights will do, and there are battery-powered movie lights that are quite portable. Like flash units, such sources must usually be used with reflectors or additional back and side lights to overcome excessive contrast and give an effect of roundness or depth to the picture.

These, however, are desperate measures to be taken only when artificial light is absolutely necessary. The most satisfactory light, as always, is daylight. It can be controlled to a surprising degree with little or no special equipment. A leafy tree branch will make a shade; a handkerchief, a diffuser; a white shirt or towel, a reflector. (A coloured shirt or towel can be a reflector for black-

and-white photography, but not for colour as it will tint the light reflected from it.) Small, bright reflectors can be made from aluminium foil. I have even used the inside of a camp frying pan, with good results. For close-ups, small mirrors like those supplied with ladies' handbags will substitute for lights. Army-type metal mirrors are a bit larger, lighter, and less breakable. Sunlight can be focused with a hand lens into as intense a beam as desired. In fact, at the focal point of the hand lens, where the intensity is at a maximum, there is a danger of incinerating the subject; the hand lens should be used farther from the subject, where the beam is wider and the intensity reduced. Lenses and mirrors can be used in conjunction to provide side or back lighting.

Supporting Equipment

Tripods are likely to be bulky, but they may be worth carrying if they have convenient controls. Recent models are of light, strong alloys developed for use in aircraft. They are shorter when folded and more rigid when opened than older models. No tripod should be considered if it does not have an elevator or movable centre post. These not only make it easy to raise and lower the camera, they can also be inverted to position the camera below the apex of the tripod for photographing flowers or other small objects at or near ground level. The ideal tripod would have cranks to move the camera forward and back and from side to side as well as up and down. Unfortunately, it has not yet been invented.

A camera clamp should always be carried, even when a tripod is also taken. The clamp must have a universal ball-and-socket joint and a screw to fit the tripod socket on the camera. The smaller clamps will fit easily into a pocket, but may not have wide enough jaws to grip some potential supports. With a clamp the camera can be mounted on any convenient object. A walking stick makes a good unipod (they eliminate vibration without being rigid) and several poles can be lashed together to improvise a tripod. The frame of a rucksack makes a good low camera support. Attaching the camera to a tree sounds like a good idea, but it isn't. Trees sway in the wind and only the lower trunk of a large tree is really stationary. It is better to drive a stake into the ground and clamp the camera to it.

Carrying the Camera

There are two schools of thought as to how cameras should be carried. One, which might be termed the *Semper paratus* school, holds that cameras should always be ready to shoot in an instant. The shutter speed and aperture should be set for the average prevailing light conditions and the lens focused at the hyperfocal distance (see Chapter 3). According to this school, the camera should be carried, if not in the hand, at least slung around the neck so that with one quick motion the photographer can raise it to his eye and shoot. Better yet, he might shoot from the hip, like Wyatt Earp.

Extremists of this school disdain the use of cases and even of lens caps, though some make the concession of using a lens cap tied to the camera with a bit of thread so it can be flipped off in an instant. The latest fashion is to carry a filter always attached to the lens to protect it.

There are no reliable statistics on the incidence of camera repairs among this group, but an informal survey by the author suggests that few worthwhile pictures are waiting to jump out at the photographer. An unprotected camera carried all day on dusty trails or snowy slopes is likely to develop trouble, and the nearest repair shop may be far away. In carrying an open camera over one's shoulder, one also risks burning a hole in a focal-plane shutter. The lens acts as a burning glass, concentrating the sun's rays on one spot on the shutter curtain (which is usually made of rubberized cloth) until it burns through. This can happen even when the person carrying the camera is moving. The result is a rounded white blob that appears in the same place on every frame. If the trip is a long one, it may appear on hundreds of pictures before it is discovered. Changing the focus to a close distance so that the image of the sun (at infinity) will not be sharp will reduce the danger somewhat, but since it defeats the instant readiness ideal, it seems better to use a lens cap. A camera case provides additional protection against dust and accidental damage.

The opposite school of camera carrying is the *Chelonia deliberatus*, or cautious tortoise school. This group holds that good pictures almost always require planning, and that protecting the camera from dust, dampness, heat, and hard knocks is more important than having it ready for instant use. Extremists of this school wrap their cameras in spare clothing and stow them in the middle of a pack or duffel bag. This results in a lot of lost picture opportunities when getting at the camera is just too much trouble.

Perhaps a middle road is best. The camera, in its case, could be carried in the top of a pack when picture-taking is not imminent and around the photographer's neck between shots. When several people are hiking together, it will be easier for the photographer to reach his camera if it is in someone else's pack rather than his own. It is a good idea to keep the camera and film in tightly closed plastic bags. If properly tied they will withstand dust and rain and even a short dunking during stream-fording or canoe-loading operations. They will not, of course, help the camera that gets stepped on by a mule.

When the camera is carried 'at the ready' it should be hung around the neck at chest level and secured against swinging by a snap like that on a dog's leash that engages a ring on the camera case. The snap is attached by a lanyard to the photographer's belt or between the shoulder straps of his pack. Fancy rigs of this type use lanyards of elastic shock cord.

Accessories should be carried in a pack or saddle-bag. Conventional gadget bags are not suitable for unmechanized travel. Once, when arriving by bush plane at a mining camp in the Canadian Arctic, I was met by several Eskimos, one of whom hoisted a large gadget bag on to his back and carried it by putting the shoulder strap across his brow like an Indian's tump-line. Brilliant as this solution is, it should not be attempted over any distance by anyone not accustomed to that method of carrying a load.

Nothing can spoil a trip to the wilds as quickly as an overload, but film is one item that should be carried in ample quantity. Nothing can add quite so much to the enjoyment of a trip, both while it is taking place and later when it is remembered, as a collection of photographs to show the stay-at-homes what they missed.

IO:

Out in the Cold

WINTER offers unique opportunities for nature photographers, but it brings a number of perplexing problems
too. Since I have had considerable experience taking
pictures in the Arctic and Antarctic, people often ask me how I
manage to work at such low temperatures. Actually, keeping the
photographer in working order is a minor problem compared to
keeping the camera and film working.

It is possible to design equipment that will function well in any
specified environment but, unfortunately, most of us have to work
with cameras, film, and accessories designed for normal temperature and humidity. Even in the temperate zones, it gets cold
enough in winter to make most cameras unreliable, if not completely inoperative.

There is a certain amount of lubrication in all cameras, usually a
'light' oil. It is light at normal room temperatures, but will act like
taffy when it gets cold enough. It is always wise to test a new
camera thoroughly before using it for serious winter shooting.
The better, newer, and more expensive cameras are lubricated
sparingly with special lubricants which do not thicken when they
get cold. But there are other problems that aren't so readily solved.

All camera mechanisms depend to some extent on springs, and
springs do not maintain the same tension at all temperatures. Then
there is the problem of contraction. The clearances between parts
in a complicated camera are rather critical. All metal contracts
slightly when cooled, but parts made of different metals will
contract at different rates and the spacing between them will
change. When a weakened spring has to push or pull against
increased friction plus sluggish lubrication it's not surprising that
the results are uncertain.

In extremely low temperatures there are even changes in the

structure and surface of the metal itself, for which there is no known cure. We can only try to avoid letting cameras get that cold. Otherwise, we must use specially designed equipment which probably will not be good for anything else.

Winterizing

Within the more usual range—down to 20°F. below zero or thereabouts—there are several steps that will help. The first is 'winterizing'. A qualified camera repair man will take the mechanism completely apart, clean it thoroughly, and reassemble it with an absolute minimum of special non-thickening lubricant. He will adjust the clearances and spring tensions to make the parts move as easily as possible, and set the shutter speeds so that they are correct when the camera is cold. They will be reasonably accurate, then, when it is warm. Winterizing, like bathing, is not permanent. It must be repeated periodically, depending on the condition of the camera and how much it is used out of doors.

If you must do your own winterizing, or advise your repair man on how to do it, the following recommendations from the U.S. Navy's Antarctic Support Force may be helpful:

Graphite lubrication or moly kote (molybdenum disulphide) is successful on irises and shutter blades but is not recommended for gears, bearings, or movie camera springs because of its affinity for moisture.

High-speed mechanisms should be lubricated with 510-50 centistroke silicone oil. All parts that operate under extreme pressure or friction should be lubricated with No. 33 light consistency silicone grease, including focusing threads, for when used in dry conditions they often are so loose that they can accidentally be moved to incorrect settings.

Any camera that is going to be out in the cold for more than a few minutes should be winterized, but that step alone does not ensure that it will work. The camera should be tested at the lowest temperature at which it will be used *before* any picture-taking is attempted and especially before any long trip during which further adjustments may be impossible. A handy way to test a camera is to put it in the refrigerator. Load it beforehand; the roll of film will be well invested. If it works well after sitting overnight in the food compartment, put it in the freezing section. If you are going to be working in really cold weather, use a picnic ice chest or insulated food bag with dry ice. It takes four to six hours for the camera to get thoroughly chilled and, of course, you will have to make the tests quickly before it warms up. Try the slow shutter speeds and the fast ones. Move all the controls. Take a few frames of an evenly-lighted blank wall at different speeds, adjusting the aperture for equivalent exposure (for example, 1/10 sec. at $f/16$, 1/50 at $f/7$, and 1/250 at $f/3.2$; or, if your aperture control has click stops, use the series 1/4 sec. at $f/22$, 1/60 sec. at $f/5.6$, 1/125 sec. at $f/4$ and 1/250 sec. at $f/2.8$). By examining the resulting nega-tives, you can answer two important questions: Is the shutter speed consistent in the different ranges? Is the exposure even throughout the frame? It is also important to wind the film all the way through the camera to check the film transport mechanism.

Cold Weather Cameras and Film

Some cameras stand cold better than others. In general, the simpler the mechanism, the less there is to freeze up. For this reason, one expert recommends that a press camera be carried on all cold assignments, if only as a spare camera. (Of course, the front shutter should be used, not the focal-plane shutter.) This is good advice, although the size and weight of the camera and its acces-sories might be prohibitive for skiing, snow-shoeing, or travelling by dog-sled.

Emil Schulthess, whose magnificent book *Antarctica* (Collins, 1961) remains the best pictorial record of that continent, says that he has found focal-plane shutters more resistant to cold than leaf shutters. In this respect his experience is the opposite of mine (and I don't think it's because he was working in the south polar area at the time I was working in the north). Before leaving Switzerland, Schulthess had his cameras completely overhauled at the factory and thoroughly tested in cold chambers. My experience has been that focal-plane shutters (the type commonly used in 35-mm. cameras) are likely to develop a lag which causes one half of the shutter to travel faster than the other, with the result that one side of the negative gets too much exposure and the other side too little. Leaf shutters, which open from the centre out, are more likely to give a uniform exposure but they tend to slow down, so that at a setting of 1/10 sec., for example, they may actually give an exposure of 1/2 sec. On twin-lens reflex cameras of the automatic type, the film-transport mechanism is more likely to freeze than is the shutter. The film will wind all right, but it won't stop at the next frame as it should.

Newer cameras are more likely to have cold-resistant lubrication, and some of the newer shutters are good at low temperatures, but old, well-worn cameras sometimes work better, because wear has increased the clearances between their moving parts. Certainly no new camera should be taken on a trip to a cold region before it has been thoroughly tested and 'run in.'

Unfortunately, the problems of photography in the cold do not end with the camera. Film is also affected. Colour films lose as much as $1\frac{1}{2}$ stops in speed at $-50°$F. Black-and-white films suffer a similar loss, and the higher the film speed the greater the loss. For this reason, among others, slow films should be used for winter shooting whenever there is enough light. It is regrettable that no tables have been published giving exposure indexes for various films at various temperatures, so that the photographer could compute exposures with a thermometer in one hand and an exposure meter in the other. Actually, in most cameras the loss of shutter speed tends to compensate to some extent for the loss in film speed, but the results are far from predictable. If precise exposures are required, tests under equivalent conditions are the only usable guide.

Film becomes brittle when cold and dry, and will crack or tear if subjected to too much strain. Roll film will sometimes chip along the edges, and sometimes break. In 35-mm. cameras the film is most likely to break if you advance the film to the end of the roll and then try to wind it some more while the end is held by the spool. Usually the sprocket holes tear first, and then the film will break along a jagged V. In the process a lot of little bits of film chip off. They have sharp corners and will scratch the film beyond redemption. Because of this danger, a roll which has been partly torn should not be rewound into the cartridge, but should be taken out of the camera in the dark and stored in a light-tight box. One of the cans in which cartridges of 35-mm. colour film are packed would be a good container for a film of that size. It should be sealed with tape to distinguish it from unused rolls and prevent accidental opening before it reaches the darkroom.

Static electricity is a serious problem under winter shooting conditions. The low temperature and humidity encourage static, and the wool and fur worn by the photographer probably add to it. The results can show as jagged streaks or rows of dots on the negative. Sometimes the static marks look like pine trees and sometimes like miniature lightning flashes (which, of course, is exactly what they are). The marks on the negative are actually the images of tiny sparks created when the film is moved. Since they are of the same nature as the picture image, there is no way to remove them once they are on the film. Sparks can be avoided by winding and re-winding the film very slowly and by doing it when the camera is warm, if you have a choice. It is better to waste a few unused frames by putting a new roll of film in the camera before going outdoors, rather than risk static marks by reloading after the camera is cold.

Static marks did not come to the attention of film manufacturers until ultra-high-speed films began to be produced in the 1950s. Presumably the problem had always been there, but earlier films were not sensitive enough to record the light from the sparks and less photography was then being done in the cold. Frantic research established that measures such as grounding the camera or humidifying the air in the developing laboratory have no real effect. There was one high-quality camera on the market then that had a glass pressure plate to hold the film in position. Naturally this camera tended to produce static marks even when it wasn't cold and ultimately the glass pressure plate had to be abandoned in favour of a metal one. Now most high-speed films have an anti-static coating which eliminates the danger at normal temperatures and reduces it even under cold, dry conditions.

The unappreciated problem of static marks was probably responsible for the superstition among old Arctic hands that the Northern Lights would somehow fog film, even through a light-tight box. This was once expounded to me in all seriousness by Peter Freuchen, who insisted that he had seen the results himself. What actually happened, I am sure, was that some early explorer found mysterious images on his film at a time when the aurora had been active and, following the age-old process by which myths have always been created, assumed a connection between the two events.

Exposure Problems

Winter sunshine, reflected by snow on the ground, can be so bright that the photographer is afraid to trust his light meter and will tend to over-expose. It has been definitely established that most light meters *do* work properly when cold (except cadmium sulphide cells, see p. 43), and the meter is a better judge of unfamiliar conditions than the eye, so it should be believed. But, as always, its information must be interpreted.

Judging contrast is more difficult than measuring the intensity of light. Contrast can be extreme under winter conditions, or it can be so reduced on overcast days that shadows are virtually eliminated. In the polar regions a combination of blowing snow, ice fog, and overcast sometimes produces a condition called 'whiteout', in which all visual reference points are lost. It becomes impossible to judge distances or perceive the snow in front of one's feet. Men have hallucinations, drive around in circles, or find themselves unable to take a step. The experience has been described as 'like being on the inside of a ping-pong ball'. (As a matter of fact, in the psychology laboratories where these conditions are reproduced experimentally, half of a real ping-pong ball is glued over each of the subject's eyes.)

Extremes of high and low contrast may even occur on the same day, and the light can go from one extreme to the other in a few minutes when a storm blows up. In both cases, determining the best exposure calls for extra care. When the sun is shining on a snowy landscape with dark rocks, trees, or people, particularly at a high altitude where the air is clear and the light intense, the range of illumination may be so great that no film could record it all. Then a compromise, entailing a sacrifice of detail in either highlights or shadows, will have to be made. The best compromise will be found by computing exposure from the highest and lowest readings (as described in Chapter 4) if it is possible to measure them.

On the other end of the scale, the extreme lack of contrast in some snowscapes makes them look dull and lifeless. There is no way of adding sparkle to the scene if it isn't there, but the snow will be a little whiter if the photographer takes his exposure reading from a medium-toned object such as his own hand, rather than from a snow bank. This is true because a reflected-light meter gives an average reading for everything within its angle of view and the exposure computer yields an exposure that will render an average as a 'middle tone' or medium grey. If everything the meter sees is white, then white will come out grey in the picture.

An incident-light meter will not necessarily give more reliable exposures. It does the same sort of averaging, but bases it on the light falling on the meter rather than that reflected from the subject. It can be misled by light reflected from the snow if the same light is not also reflected on to the subject. It assumes that the subject is medium grey in tone, which may not be so if the subject is a snow-covered peak or the mouth of a cave.

A dark subject surrounded by white snow will be under-exposed if the exposure is measured from the snow, as it will be if an over-all reflected-light reading is used. On the other hand, an exposure based on the subject alone may over-expose the snow and reduce its appearance of texture. Experience is always the best guide to the interpretation of meter readings, and in snow scenes it is indispensable.

Snow is very blue (as everyone knows who has ever been inside a snow cave and seen light filtering through it). The light from a blue sky is also very blue and the shadows on snow are intensely blue. There is also a lot of ultra-violet in sky light and snow. Films are sensitive to ultra-violet, which is invisible to us, and they are more sensitive to blue than is the human eye. Consequently, blue shadows will appear almost white in a black-and-white picture, reducing the texture of the snow and obscuring its shape. In colour pictures the U-V will often produce a slight haze over the entire picture, and the predominance of blue will give the picture a bluish cast.

Snow scenes should always be photographed through a filter to block the ultra-violet and correct for the excess blue. In black-and-white a medium yellow filter is the lightest that should be used. An orange filter is usually better and red is sometimes indicated. In colour a 'sky-light' filter is the usual choice. These filters are ordinarily thought of as controlling the rendering of the sky, but in winter scenes they do much more; they control the texture and colour of the scene even if the sky is not included. They should be used even on overcast days because although the sky may not be blue it is still radiating ultra-violet.

High-speed films should not be used for well-lighted subjects in any climate. They are especially inappropriate for snowscapes because of their poor tolerance for cold and for over-exposure. But where low temperature and low light levels occur together, as in the polar twilight period, they may be the best choice. Polaroid films, incidentally, can be exposed in the cold but cannot be developed satisfactorily unless they are warm.

Any situation where there is a lot of light calls for extra care in loading and unloading the camera. If no shade is available take off your coat, put the camera inside, and reach through the sleeves to insert and remove the film.

Other Cold Weather Problems

The best, and the only reliable, solution to the various problems of shooting in the cold is to keep the camera and film warm. They need not be as warm as they would be in summer, but just warm enough to ensure that they work reliably. The best way to carry a camera in winter is inside your coat. I have seen skiers tearing down icy slopes amid clouds of snow with cameras slung over their shoulders, whipping in the breeze. They cut a dashing figure, but I doubt that they get many pictures. (I have had my Eskimo parka fitted with a zipper so I can carry cameras inside, around my neck.) If you travel by car, keep the camera inside with you, not in the trunk. If you use a gadget bag, keep it on the floor near the heater. If you travel by air, don't pack cameras in your baggage; it may be stowed in an unheated compartment.

Pocket hand warmers are a convenient source of warmth away from mechanical heat sources. They will work only in a confined space, because they depend on the vapour given off by lighter fluid, and the fluid will not vaporize if it gets too cold. But one or two hand warmers carried inside a gadget bag will keep the cameras and film warm well into the sub-zero range. Sometimes it is also helpful to carry hand warmers in your shirt pockets and sling a camera around your neck, under your coat.

Whatever source of heat you use, the camera should be taken

out only when you are ready to shoot, and put away again as soon as possible. Sometimes, of course, this is impossible, as when the camera must be set up long in advance and operated either automatically or by remote control. The set-ups in which wild animals or birds trip the shutter and take their own pictures are a case in point.

Any arrangement which allows the camera to stand idle and exposed to the cold for a long time invites shutter trouble. In addition, set-ups that use batteries as a source of energy for tripping the shutter or powering flash units, or both, are prone to battery trouble. As the temperature drops the chemical reaction by which dry cells manufacture current gets slower, and therefore devices which drain a lot of energy from dry cells get sluggish and finally quit. A flash unit which recharges in 3 seconds at room temperature may take a minute or more at 10° below zero and probably won't work at all below that. Wet cells (the type of battery used in cars) will operate down to the freezing point of the fluid in them, which varies with the proportion of acid to water, but is usually low enough to be quite safe. But wet cells are not made in many of the sizes needed for photo equipment. Common sense suggests that any photographer venturing into cold regions with battery-operated equipment should carry a meter for checking the batteries, preferably one that will show how they behave under a load.

Other parts of electrical equipment are likely to go haywire. The tripping circuits of flash units sometimes develop leaks so that some of them will not flash at all, while others will go off by themselves every minute or so. In one case I made use of such a self-firing unit by timing the cycle and opening the camera shutter just before the light triggered itself. But I do not recommend such a procedure except for emergencies.

Here again, the only real solution is to keep the cameras and any associated electrical equipment *including batteries* warm enough to function normally. Where electrical power is available, the equipment can be wrapped in insulating material and kept warm with an electric heating pad or blanket. Some military cameras have been fitted with electrically-heated jackets, and these occasionally turn up on the surplus market. They are usually designed to work on 24 volts d.c., the output of two modern vehicle batteries in series. I cannot think of any reason why the electrically heated flying suits and socks which are sold by surplus stores could not be adapted

[19] *Great White Heron taking off. Photographed in the Florida Keys.*
(See page 154 dealing with timing.)

[20] *Adélie penguin on the march from nest to feeding ground.*

[21] *Marine animals from the ocean floor under permanent shelf ice in Antarctica. Photographed in a refrigerated aquarium.*

[22] *Leopard seal in the Antarctic. Photographed by Prof. Dr. Heinz Janetschek with a convertible telephoto lens. (See page 115.)*

for camera use as long as the heating elements are intact. Hand warmers will work well in an enclosed, but not air-tight, case. (Felt is an ideal material for such a case.) There are also chemical heating pads that get warm when water is added to them and will continue to generate warmth for six hours or so.

The photographer who must work both indoors and out, and go back and forth frequently, really needs two separate sets of cameras. On this, Schulthess and I agree. A cold camera suddenly brought into a warm, humid room is a frightening sight. First moisture condenses on all the glass and metal surfaces, clouding the lens like a cataract in an eye, and then the moisture freezes. There is no safe way of removing it from the outside and no way at all of removing it from the parts inside the camera, where the same thing happens. The only solution is to wait, sometimes for several hours, until the camera warms up completely, and the moisture evaporates. (People who wear spectacles have the same trouble with them.) Even if the camera has been kept relatively warm while outside, the difference may be enough to cause trouble. The best procedure is to use one camera indoors and another outside, keeping the outside one where it will not get too cold but where it will not be subjected to a sudden rise in temperature. When a camera is brought indoors it should be allowed to warm up gradually, protected by a moisture-tight plastic bag inside of a gadget bag or case. Most buildings in cold regions are quite cold at floor level. (If a pencil is dropped on the floor it may not be possible to pick it up until spring.) Therefore, the best place to store a camera while it warms up is down near the floor, preferably under a bunk where no one can step on it.

Unprotected skin will stick to cold metal, and tends to remain with the metal instead of with the person to whom it belongs. No one is likely to try operating a camera with bare hands in extreme cold, but the metal around the viewing window is more of a problem. Many cameras must be held close to the eye for the photographer to see what he is getting. Eyebrows and eyelids will sometimes stick to the metal. The best solution for this problem is to cover the metal around the window with masking or adhesive tape. It also helps to keep the camera in the type of case that can be left on while it is being used. The case keeps the camera away from the skin.

The photographer's breath will condense on cold surfaces—

metal or glass—and the mist will turn to ice if it is cold enough. It is usually necessary for him to hold his breath while the camera is in front of his face or take care to breathe in a different direction. Sun glasses are often necessary not only for comfort but also to prevent snow blindness, and the camera may deflect breath on to the glasses and fog them. Of course, sun glasses that have metal rims should not be considered. The type of goggle that has a soft rubber rim and seals tight around the eyes will keep the breath from condensing on the inside.

It is dangerous to wipe or scrape frost from a lens—it may scratch the glass or coating. Blown snow or very light condensation can be brushed off with a soft, camel-hair brush. The brush should be carried in an outside pocket to keep it cold and dry. The type of brush that folds into its handle like a lady's lipstick is the most convenient to carry.

No camera on the market can be operated properly by a man wearing mittens. This is inconvenient, but not likely to be changed. I wear thin gloves inside mittens. Even in very cold weather I can take the mittens off long enough to work the camera with gloves on.

From all this it may sound as if the best advice would be to leave the camera at home until spring. Nothing could be further from the truth. Many ordinary subjects become exciting pictures in winter, and recording them is well worth the few precautions it requires. In particular, snow is the photographer's friend. By subduing details it emphasizes lines and contours; it increases colour and brightness contrast, and it reflects light into shadows. It can make a strong composition out of a scene that would be confusing and 'busy' in summer.

And photography probably offers the only acceptable excuse for the nature fan who wants to be outdoors in winter. Indoor types are accustomed to the idea that we who take pictures are all a little barmy, and that seemingly irrational behaviour is normal among us. So when one wants to go for a bracing hike in a blizzard, it's convenient to be able to say, 'Oh, I think I'll just go out and take a few pictures.'

Underwater Photography

I WAS prowling peacefully along a rocky shore, collecting mussels for dinner, when I heard a splash. Just beyond the outer line of rocks I saw a column of water vapour shoot into the air, like the spout of a whale, but in miniature. A glistening black object broke the surface. It floated for a minute and then, instead of diving, it started moving slowly toward shore. As it approached I could see that it was about the size of a porpoise and had a bright, fluorescent yellow stripe along the water line. As it pulled itself up on the beach the eyes came into sight. They were about four inches in diameter and were located on the ventral surface one behind the other! The creature got up on its hind flippers and waddled awkwardly toward me. It was my friend Martin in his new skin-diving suit. The upper eye was his face mask and the lower one the port of a camera housing strapped to his chest.

'I got some wonderful pictures,' said Martin, '. . . if they come out.'

How that phrase took me back in memory! It had been years since I'd wondered whether a picture would 'come out'. But when I started taking underwater pictures myself I found that no thought could possibly be more appropriate.

Underwater photography went through a tremendous vogue in the 1950s. Photographers, apparently suffering a mass attack of Cousteau's 'rapture of the deep', took to the swimming pools in shoals. Everything was photographed underwater—telephones, automobiles, male models in drip-dry suits, pretty girls in bathing suits, pretty girls without bathing suits, housewives pretending to make toast, and children pretending to drink soda pop. Most of these pictures were not remarkably good, but it was remarkable that they could be taken at all. They attracted attention, and that was what they were supposed to do. By now everyone has seen pictures made underwater, the hucksters have moved on to other gimmicks, and underwater photographers can get on with the business of photographing things that really belong to the undersea world.

Underwater Conditions

Stepping into the sea with mask or goggles is very much like entering the world behind the looking glass. The silvery barrier which seems so thin and yet so formidable opens only enough to let one pass, and closes immediately. The undersea world *is* breathtaking, and before long you want to take pictures of it. Then comes the rude discovery that when you enter that alien world you also step back in time to the dawn of photography.

We have become used to the fact that in air the camera can photograph anything the eye can see—and often more. It can cut through fog; it can look a fly in the eye; it can bring distant subjects closer. Almost anything you want the camera to do can be done—if you have the money for accessories. Almost any technical information you may want is published in handbooks.

In that other world below the surface, everything is different. The experts still build much of their own equipment, by hand. (When did you last build a camera?) There are no reliable tables of exposure, filter factors, development times, or any of the other things we have come to take for granted. What tables *have* been published hold good only for the waters where they were derived, and the only sound recommendation you will get is to make a test and see if it comes out. If it does, you still won't know much because underwater optical conditions change from day to day and even from hour to hour.

And underwater the camera can see much *less* than the eye. This is partly because we have two eyes and can therefore concentrate on things at one particular distance and ignore what is in front of and behind that point, but a larger factor is the marvellous ability of the mind to perceive shapes and organize visual clues. The eye can detect minute differences in colour and texture. The perception of motion helps too. Many forms of marine life are so camouflaged as to be invisible until they move. Needless to say, they are completely invisible in a still photograph. The only way to photograph them is to get them against a different background— one that they don't match. A sting ray lying on the bottom is virtually impossible to see in a photograph, but a ray swimming can be seen from the side against a background of water, or from below against the surface.

When we pick up rocks or sea shells at the shore and take them home they seem somehow to lose their lustre. The same is true of the wonders we try to capture on film. I am afraid the truth is that just as the eye can see underwater only a fraction of what it could see on land, so the camera underwater can record only a fraction of what the eye can see. Water clear enough for top-notch undersea photography is found in only a few places in the world's oceans, and even there, only at certain times.

The water is very clear in the Bahamas and there are enormous stretches of white sandy bottom at 20 feet or less that reflect light and give a beautifully rounded illumination. Marine life, however, is not as abundant there as in waters that offer more food and more concealment. When the movie *20,000 Leagues Under the Sea* was filmed there, whole undersea gardens were brought in and set up by prop men. Even so, the film company sat around for several weeks waiting for good weather.

In the Florida Keys there is more to photograph and the water can be very clear at times. May and June are the best months. But all coral shores undergo a continual 'snowfall' of minute particles of eroded coral. The slightest wind stirs up the bottom enough to prohibit picture-taking, and a severe storm will cover the undersea landscape with two or three inches of silt. One day in five may be a good day for underwater photography.

The best conditions are found in the eastern Mediterranean, where the water is as clear as laboratory distilled water, and in certain large springs where the fresh water is free from organic or mineral sediment. Many of the 'gimmick' pictures of the early underwater period were taken in these springs, and some of the undersea adventures shown on television are filmed there. Any marine life shown is, of course, filmed separately. The threatening sharks and octopi are photographed in an aquarium.

Have you ever wondered why we do not see any overall pictures of the sunken Spanish galleons that writers are so fond of describing? The answer, I suspect, is that no camera can see from one end of such a ship to the other. It may almost be taken as a fundamental law that there are no long shots under water.

These discouraging facts are forced on us by the nature of the medium. Water is much less transparent than air, and natural bodies of water (as distinct from swimming pools or aquariums where the water is filtered) contain quantities of minute particles in suspension. Some of these are plants, some are animals, and some are bits of sand, mud, or coral, but they all impede the passage of light. Some of the particles absorb light (actually they convert its energy into heat) and others reflect or scatter it. Scattering is more of a problem for the photographer than absorption. It produces the same effect that heavy dust clouds or thick fog do in air. There may be plenty of light and still it may be impossible to see more than a few feet.

Overcoming Flatness

Because of the difficulty of recording any distant background and because the photographer must work as close to the subject as possible, most underwater pictures appear flat. They are not only flat in the photographic sense—the images lack contrast between light and dark tones—but also are flat in the sense that they do not look three dimensional.

To overcome photographic flatness, a fairly energetic developer should be used for black-and-white films. Developing times should be 10 per cent to 20 per cent longer than usual. Although it seems like a good idea to use a slow film because such films have higher inherent contrast than fast ones, it is probably better in actual practice to use a medium-fast film in shallow water and a fast film in deep water so that the lens aperture can be kept small to overcome difficulties in focusing. It is not really practicable to increase contrast in colour, but fortunately this is not usually necessary.

There are other tricks for overcoming the other kind of flatness—the lack of apparent depth—although, of course, these tricks do not really restore what the low visibility takes away. Framing is the most effective technique. This means having a dark object in the near foreground at the edge or edges of the picture. Shooting through a hole in a coral or between two rocks is a good way to achieve this effect. The best way is to shoot from inside an underwater cave, but since caves are frequented by moray eels and other unfriendly creatures, I would hesitate to advise any readers to back into them.

Another useful technique for simulating depth is backlighting. This means simply having the light come from behind the subject. It is frequently impossible, of course, but it is usually worth trying. Shooting up at an angle toward the surface is one way; photographing fish in the shadow of your boat is another. These same tricks—framing and backlighting—are useful above water, too, especially where the air is dusty or foggy. They have been used in many of the best pictures of rodeos, marine mists, and London streets.

Filters to Correct Imbalance in Colour

Increased exposure will not help to penetrate underwater murk because the film will record the scattered light instead of the image we want to see. In fact, a minimal exposure and extended development are best. Filters will improve the situation a bit. The suspended particles scatter more blue and green than other colours, so a yellow or orange filter will reduce the intensity of scattered light somewhat and allow more of the image to show. But no filter will get the particles themselves out of the way.

When shooting in colour, filters can be used only sparingly— just enough to restore the balance of the different colours that make up white light. The filters used for colour, therefore, will not help much in penetrating underwater haze. Colour does help, however, by making the subject stand out and by increasing the feeling of depth. For this reason, colour pictures are often better than black-and-white photographs of the same subjects, but the shooting conditions must be better for colour to succeed at all.

Only if the water appears *exceptionally* clear to the eye will it seem less than opaque to the camera, and even then the best technique is to move in as close to the subject as possible in order to minimize the number of particles between it and the camera.

Focusing Underwater

The amount of solid matter suspended in the water varies with time and place. The problem of refraction, however, is the same in all waters. Refraction is the phenomenon that accounts for the apparent 'bending' at the water line of a stick thrust into the water. Rays of light pass first through the water and then through the air inside the container before they reach the lens. As they pass from one transparent medium to the other, the rays are bent outward, making everything underwater appear larger and closer than it would on the surface, which accounts for the extraordinary size of sea monsters and fish that got away. This effect fools the

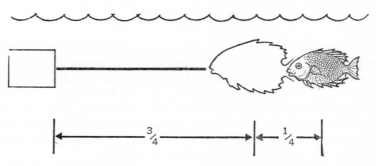

Fig. 21 Apparent and real distance underwater. To the observer and the camera, the subject looks one fourth nearer and larger than it really is. Thus, the camera would have to be focused at 3 feet for a subject actually at 4 feet.

camera as well as the eye. A fish that appears to be 3 feet away will be photographed in focus if the camera is focused at 3 feet, but the actual measured distance will be 4 feet (Fig. 21). The scattering and absorption of light, however, occurs throughout the full 4 feet of water between camera and subject. The definition and contrast of the image decreases rapidly as the actual distance increases, so the clearest pictures will call for a short actual working distance and an even shorter apparent distance. Here is where trouble usually starts.

Many common types of cameras have a minimum focusing distance of 3 feet in air. Underwater this visual distance of 3 feet means an actual, measured distance of 4 feet, which is frequently too far for a satisfactory picture. Furthermore, the depth of field and size of the field will correspond to the apparent distance of 3 feet, not the actual distance. It may be necessary to back up to include the whole subject, and that will decrease the visibility.

Another way of expressing this is to say that the lens acts as though its focal length were increased by one third. The usual lens for a 35-mm. camera has a focal length of 50 mm. in air; underwater its *effective* focal length is 67 mm. and its depth of field and angle of view are those of a 67-mm. lens. This is a bit long, but not impossibly so.

It is difficult to focus accurately underwater, especially since the photographer and subject may be drifting in currents. A small aperture is usually necessary to obtain depth of field. A small image will have greater depth of field than a large one at any given lens aperture and is therefore preferable. This means, in turn, that the 35-mm. camera is the most useful type of camera for underwater photography. It has a short lens to begin with, and on the better ones an even shorter (wide-angle) lens can be substituted for the normal one. If the camera design permits, a lens of 25- to 35-mm. focal length is desirable underwater.

Another overwhelmingly persuasive reason for choosing a 35-mm. camera is the number of pictures it will take before reloading. Remember that in order to change film one will first have to surface, then take off his mask and breathing apparatus, dry his hands and camera housing, remove anywhere from one to fifteen bolts, and finally extract the camera *before* he starts the normal reloading routine. The ordinary load for 35-mm. cameras is a 20- or 36-exposure cartridge. Many of the better 35-mm. cameras have accessory backs that accept 50-foot rolls of film and allow several hundred exposures before reloading.

The directions that come with the film say 'always reload in subdued light, never in direct sunlight'. This is good advice, but hard to follow in a pitching rowing-boat anchored off shore. The height of efficiency (and luxury) would be to have two identical camera outfits and a dry-handed assistant in the boat overhead to reload one camera while the other was being used.

Camera Housings

Underwater housings come in a variety of futuristic shapes and materials. They look fancy, but compared with modern cameras they are crude. The RolleiMarin housing for the Rolleiflex, designed by Hans Hass, an expert diver, is one of the few that can really be operated conveniently underwater, and it is perhaps the only housing with which a diver wearing a mask can actually see what he is getting on film. It has three main disadvantages: the Rollei lens is too long; the camera will take only 12 frames, after which the apparatus must be brought to the surface and the case opened to reload; and the greatest drawback, for many people, is the price of about £130, which does not include the camera.

In the 'under £100' class, an expensive housing is not necessarily better than an inexpensive one. The cheapest type of all is a soft plastic bag with a circular glass port at one end. All the various controls on the camera can be operated through the plastic while submerged, an advantage that cannot be claimed by many housings costing much more. The heavier, cast-metal housings are watertight to greater depths, but this is a dubious advantage because there is not enough light to take pictures at those depths anyway, unless artificial light is used. A housing that is watertight to 250 feet and has no flash connections is a waste of money. With many of these housings, the shutter speed and aperture can be changed only after opening the housing. This means that the photographer has to make a preliminary descent to take a meter reading—a sealed fruit jar makes a good meter housing—then surface to set the camera, then dive again to take the picture. By that time the subject may have departed.

Even less convenient, most inexpensive housings have no mechanism for focusing the camera and no way of seeing when it is in focus. They thus transform an expensive camera into the equivalent of a box camera. True, the lens is faster, but if it can't be focused the lens has to be stopped down for greatest depth of field, so the lens speed is wasted.

Watertight Cameras

It is more sensible to buy a box camera in the first place. There is an underwater box camera, the Mako Shark, selling in the U.S.A. for $15. It is made entirely of plastic and the camera forms its own housing. Like a terrestrial box camera, it uses roll film. The shutter speed, focus, and aperture are fixed but the sensitivity can be controlled to some extent by using films of different speeds. This camera will do almost everything that an expensive one will do and it has one great advantage—if the case leaks nothing will be ruined but one roll of film.

Making the camera itself watertight, instead of enclosing it in a watertight housing, is a very sound idea. The size and buoyancy (the underwater reciprocal of weight) can be greatly reduced and it is much easier to operate the camera and change the film. One watertight camera, formerly called the Calypso, is now issued under the name of Nikonos by the Nikon people. The Japanese manufacturers have kindly provided the following description:

The camera has been specifically designed and constructed to be perfectly water-tight, enabling us to use it not only without an additional watertight case under the water down to a depth of about 150 feet but also without any care under difficult conditions where the camera is likely to be exposed to water, rain, snow, sand, mud, dust cloud (radio-active or not), high degree of humidity, etc. Therefore, the NIKONOS will seriously be required and advantageously be used by aqualung divers, sailors, salvagers, fishermen, shipbuilders, etc. for underwater photography, news-cameramen, policemen at the inundation, rain storm, fire, etc., yachtmen canoeist, anglers, hunters, mountain climbers, skiers, skaters, sea-bathers, as well as by surgeons, scientific and industrial engineers, naturalist, surveyors, speleologist, explorers, etc.

Such a camera is also useful in air where the camera may get splattered or drenched. The camera will not be harmed, but it should be remembered that it cannot take clear pictures with drops of water on the faceplate. All the controls on this camera can be operated from the outside, although the knobs are rather small. It is claimed that the camera can be sterilized (but not with the film in it) for medical use. The viewfinder would be very difficult to use while wearing a face mask, so an accessory open-frame viewfinder is a necessity underwater. It costs about £75 in Great Britain.

Its main disadvantage is that it has neither range finder nor reflex focusing system. The distance to the subject must be measured or estimated. If it is measured, it must be corrected for refraction by setting the camera for $\frac{3}{4}$ of the measured distance. A more practical procedure is to set the camera for an average distance, use a small aperture, and try to stay within the depth of field. The focus can be changed underwater.

Shallow-water Housings

Another radical, but highly practical, suggestion is not to take the camera underwater at all but to shoot instead through something like a glass-bottomed bucket. A sophisticated version of this versatile instrument can be built with a rectangular glass bottom the same shape as the negative (Fig. 22). A mount can be installed to hold the camera so that its field of view exactly corresponds to the window, and the whole box can be aimed as a unit. Any ordinary range finder or reflex viewing system can be used for focusing because the refraction that distorts distances underwater affects these systems just as it affects the picture. Since the air in the box makes it very buoyant it will be hard to control unless weights are attached around the bottom. A focusing cloth or hood is usually necessary to prevent reflections of the sky on the window.

Users of reflex cameras might try a variation of such a box with the window in the side instead of in the bottom (Fig. 22). The camera is placed on the bottom and pointed out through the window. The photographer looks down into the ground-glass screen. The box must be big enough so that the operator can reach down into it and work the camera's controls.

Of course these boxes and buckets can be used only to photograph objects that are near the surface, but most good picture possibilities occur in this zone. The light falls off rapidly as we go down, and the colour of the light changes, growing more and more blue-green. As I have mentioned, these effects vary greatly from one time and place to another, so it is impossible to make up any useful tables. But the marine life we are interested in photographing depends on sunlight, too, and most of it is to be found in shallow water.

Artificial Light

Below about 20 feet—the exact depth varies with the clarity of the water—natural light becomes too faint to use and the photographer must depend on bulb or electronic flash. These sources work nicely underwater if enclosed in suitable housings, but the pictures taken with them usually exhibit all the disadvantages of terrestrial flash pictures, magnified. The foreground is unnaturally bright while the background is dark; textures are subdued where they should be brought out; and the shadows are in all the wrong places.

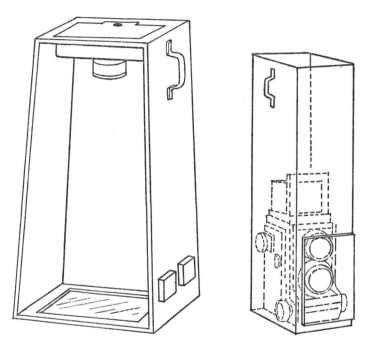

Fig. 22 Shallow-water camera housings.

The best solution is to keep the flash away from the camera. Some flash units have telescoping arms that can be extended, but they are difficult to manoeuvre and even harder to swim with. It is often helpful to have a second diver to hold the flash. Directing him is a problem since he can't hear your instructions and you have to rely on hand signals. Since no one should ever dive alone, anyway, the photographer might as well put his companion to work unless (Heaven forbid!) he is taking pictures too.

Summary

Despite its many difficulties, underwater photography can be an exciting experience, and the results can be impressive, as many published examples prove. The best underwater pictures become truly miraculous when one comes to appreciate the obstacles that were overcome to make them. Most experts, if they really let their hair down, would agree that the 'secrets' of successful underwater photography are these:

1. Work in shallow water. In many of the best photographs, the surface of the sea is just out of the frame.
2. Shoot only at close distances. The long shot probably won't come out.
3. Take plenty of time. Practice using your equipment in a swimming pool or at the beach before you go farther out.
4. Try to shoot at the best times. Make careful tests and have them developed as you work.

Finally, don't expect too much—one good picture a day is a high output.
But that one picture can be worth it.

12:

Hides and Traps

A HIDE is an enclosure designed to conceal the photographer and his apparatus. A trap, in the sense used here, is an arrangement by which the subject takes its own picture. Of the two, hides are much more useful, as we shall see.

Many of the best pictures of wild animals have been taken from hides. In recent years the development of long lenses and high-speed films has shifted the emphasis to pictures taken at long range. Nevertheless, the hide remains a most useful accessory for the nature photographer.

In the early days of nature photography, elaborate attempts were made to disguise hides as natural objects. Now we know that this is not necessary. Animals suspect any hide because of its smell. Birds will become accustomed to any new object—no matter what its shape—and will eventually lose their fear of it if it does not make threatening motions.

Birds are much more wary of motion than of shape. A loose piece of cloth flapping in the wind will frighten most birds. They have very good eyesight (as is obvious to anyone who has ever seen a hawk hunting), but they are not greatly worried about events that do not seem to be concerned with them.

Motor Vehicles

By now most birds have become accustomed to motor vehicles, and in many places a car or jeep will serve as a most convenient hide, as well as a means of transportation. Some of the more wary species, however, will accept vehicles only when they are moving, and will scatter if the car stops. The best technique then is to have an assistant drive the car as slowly as the birds will tolerate while you shoot. This is one way of making photography a team enterprise.

Naturally, a long lens and quick eye are necessary to photograph from a moving vehicle. The camera should be held so that it does not touch any part of the vehicle; in that way the photographer's muscles will absorb the vibration. (The same rule applies, incidentally, when photographing from aircraft.) Most people will find the minimum shutter speed that will yield sharp negatives under such conditions to be about 1/250 sec., but the speed will depend on the length of the lens as well as the steadiness of the photographer's arm. Motion is magnified to the same degree as is the image; a long lens must therefore be held steadier than a short one, and when the camera is in motion the long lens will require a faster shutter speed than a short one.

It should scarcely be necessary to point out that no-one should ever attempt to photograph from the roof of a moving vehicle unless it is provided with a secure, high railing. The most famous photographer of animals of our time, Ylla, was killed when she was thrown from a jeep while photographing a bullock race in India.

A few birds will accept a motionless vehicle as long as people do not emerge from it. In such cases it is very helpful to have a camera support in the car. A small tripod can be set up in many cars if two legs are extended to rest on the floor while the third is shortened to rest on a seat. In many station wagons a tripod can be set up in the conventional manner in the back. This is the best location, because the back window gives a wider unobstructed sweep than any other. The window should, of course, be opened.

The photographer should be provided with a comfortable seat from which to work—not just for his own comfort but for the sake of sharp pictures. Holding an uncomfortable position for any length of time will make his hands shake. Even with the camera on a tripod he may be unable to operate it smoothly.

Stationary Hides

A more permanent hide is better, of course, when a series of pictures are to be taken over a period of time. It is a necessity for very shy creatures that may take days to become accustomed to it.

[23] *A lion in the New York Zoo. Many zoos now have enclosures without bars, providing a convenient way to gain experience in animal photography. A large aperture was used to throw the background out of focus (see page 157).*

[24] *White-tailed deer in the forest. When photographing a wild animal, a wise photographer will start taking pictures while still at a distance and keep on shooting as he moves closer (see page 82).*

Sometimes a hide is set up at a distance and moved closer each day. In other cases a permanent hide may be left in place for weeks or years.

The usual demountable type of hide is similar to a small tent. It usually need not be waterproof, since it will not be used on rainy days, but the material must be sufficiently opaque so that subjects will not see the photographer moving about inside. Material of a neutral colour that will blend with the surroundings is probably an advantage, Here again, the photographer should be able to sit in comfort; otherwise he will not be able to stay mentally alert and physically relaxed.

In most places, a hide should protect the photographer against mosquitoes. It should also have adequate ventilation, as a hide exposed to the sun can become insufferably hot. Openings covered with nylon mosquito netting should admit air near the bottom of the hide and let it out near the top. The opening through which the lens projects can be provided with a drawstring or elastic ring to make a mosquito-proof closure.

The best way to keep a hide cool is to place it in the shade. If there are no trees at hand, a separate 'fly' (an extra cloth roof over the regular one with an open air space between) will make the enclosure more livable. Tent roofs coated with aluminium paint to reflect heat have not turned out in practice to be of any advantage.

It is not too difficult to make or have made a hide such as I have described, but it is easier to buy a small tent and convert it for use as a hide by inserting camera ports and observation peepholes. There is a dome-shaped tent which has a simple frame that fits into sleeves sewn into the tent. The inside space is not obstructed by poles, and there are no shiny metal gadgets on the outside to scare away the wildlife. Tents that have a lot of loose hooks, springs, and lengths of metal tubing, should be avoided—not only as hides but for any purpose. All tents should be staked down to prevent wind from blowing them over, advertising to the contrary notwithstanding.

The bolder birds, such as those that live along the seashore, will forget about a photographer once he is settled in his hide. Some of the more wary species, however, will not relax until they are convinced that the hide is uninhabited. To deceive them, a confederate is enlisted to walk to the hide with the photographer and then leave a few seconds later. Most birds are not conscious of any difference between the two humans entering the hide and one human leaving it. There are cases on record, however, of birds that could count up to six men entering a hide and would wait until every one had left before returning to the vicinity.

For photographing high nests or arboreal animals, a hide can be built in a tree. It is best to construct a small platform at a place where several limbs join the trunk. The hide can then be set up using the platform as a floor, and the trunk and perhaps higher branches as supports for the hide. It is best to choose a large tree, stay close to the central trunk, and not to go higher than necessary

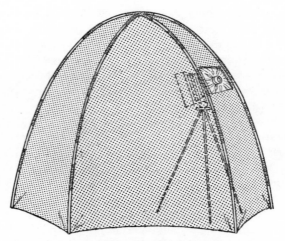

Fig. 23 A simple hide for photography in the field.

because even a very large tree will move enough in the wind to blur a picture. It may be necessary, also, to brace or tie down the branch that is to be the scene of the picture.

Land animals are sometimes more difficult to deceive than birds. They rely more on smell than on vision, and can therefore be approached most successfully from down wind.

Hides for photographing animals are usually placed at water holes or on trails the animals are known to frequent. Sometimes an artificial attraction is provided—food, salt, or water. The animals may avoid the hide at first, but will usually get used to it in time. The sense of smell that is so well developed in animals is offset, to some extent, by their curiosity and they will often come around to investigate an unfamiliar object. Usually it will be just as the photographer, after a day of fruitless waiting, has dismantled his camera and is preparing to leave.

Most animals make themselves scarce in the middle of the day. Early morning is the best time to look for them; late afternoon is second best, except for nocturnal ones. Most large animals, such as deer, are used to watching for danger at about their own level. They will rarely look for it over their heads, and will often fail to see a hide in a tree. The same is true, incidentally, of humans. People will rarely notice someone above their own eye level.

Because a high viewpoint is not often desirable for pictures of animals, the elevated hide is most useful in a remote-control arrangement where the camera is set up near the ground and the photographer operates it from a vantage point some distance away. This arrangement is intermediate between a hide and a trap, in that the photographer can see what he is photographing, even though he is not at the camera.

Remote Control

Early works on nature photography describe how the camera shutter could be tripped with a thread strung out to where the photographer lay hidden, and cautioned that the thread should be run through a screw eye at the bottom of one leg of the tripod, so that a tug on the thread would not pull the camera over. After making one exposure, the photographer had to emerge from his hide to reload the camera and cock the shutter for another try. By that time the subject was likely to be far away. The thread system has other disadvantages: a tug on the cord is likely to shake the camera, the thread stretches and causes a delay between the time it is pulled and the time the shutter opens, and it is difficult to gauge the tension necessary to open the shutter.

Fortunately, we now have a variety of devices to make the remote operation of cameras and lights as simple and as automatic as we choose. The simplest device is an air release. This is a reel of thin plastic tubing with a squeeze bulb at one end and a plunger at the other. The plunger end screws into the cable-release socket of the camera and the photographer squeezes the bulb.

Slightly more sophisticated is the electrically operated solenoid. A solenoid is an electro-magnet with a movable core. In the early decades of the flashbulb era they were used to synchronize camera shutters with flash bulbs. The flash bulb takes a certain length of time to reach full brilliance after the electric power is applied to it. The time varies according to the type of bulb. In the early synchronized bulbs, called Type M, it was 20 milliseconds (1/50 sec.). In order to have the shutter at full opening when the light from the flash reached its peak, it was necessary to delay the opening of the shutter after power was applied to the bulb. This was accomplished by connecting a solenoid to the flash circuit and having the solenoid operate the shutter. Solenoid synchronizers were made obsolete by the development of shutters with internal delay mechanisms and by electronic flash, which needs no delay.

Solenoids are still available, and are now finding new uses in remote-control photography. The simplest ones screw into a standard cable-release socket. They can be operated from any distance by simply adding more wire. The power applied must be sufficient to overcome the resistance of the wire and deliver enough energy at the solenoid to operate it reliably. Two or three flashlight batteries will be sufficient at short distances; for longer distances use a B/C ('Battery-Capacitor') flash gun, which delivers a quick surge of energy from a capacitor that has been charged by a 22½-volt battery. At very great distances higher voltages may be necessary.

When the camera is remotely operated it can, in turn, operate flash bulbs or electronic flash if it is equipped with flash connections. The batteries that power the lights should be close to the lights so that no loss of power is involved there. Electronic flash, of course, has the advantage that it will repeat its performance without replacement of bulbs. But what about the problem of changing the film?

Here we get to specialized equipment. There are several cameras that will advance the film and wind the shutter automatically after each exposure, among them the Robot, the Tessina, and the no-longer-made Foton. There are a number of cameras for which accessory motors—either spring-driven or electric—are available.

Most of these cameras use 35-mm. film but some of the more expensive ones, designed for technical recording, use 70-mm. stock. For applications where the ordinary 36-exposure cassette is not enough, there are accessory backs that take 50-foot rolls of film.

The ultimate in remote control is a radio-operated tripping device available for several cameras. It eliminates the wires from the camera to the photographer's hideout, and makes it possible for him to operate the camera from several miles away. Presumably he could even hover overhead in a helicopter. Radio-control units have not worked as well as expected in places where there is a lot of electrical interference. They have been tried and abandoned at prize fights and political conventions—but out in the open they ought to work well.

Night Photography

Hides and remote-control set-ups can be used to photograph nocturnal species whose habits are sufficiently well known that the camera or hide can be located where they are likely to appear. A water hole in a dry climate is an obvious location.

The question that usually comes to mind first is: How will the photographer see what he is doing? Ideally, he should set up all his equipment while it is still light, and he should be sufficiently familiar with it to be able to operate it in the dark. (Otherwise, he should not be using it in a hide, anyway.) As for seeing when the subject arrives in front of the camera, well, anyone who has spent many nights out of doors should know it is rarely so dark that a human cannot see after his eyes become adapted.

At permanent or long-term hide sites it may be possible to leave a small light on until the subjects get used to it. Many nocturnal animals show surprisingly little fear of lights at night and will enter a pool of light if they have sufficient motivation. Even more surprising, many animals will return to an attractive spot even after having had flash bulbs fired at them, and even though the scent of man is in the air.

If the light used to make the picture is too disturbing to the subjects, it is possible to use infra-red instead. The camera is loaded with infra-red-sensitive film and special red flash bulbs or red filters over the flash reflectors are used. This is the technique used for photographing people in dark movie theatres or for setting traps in which burglars take their own pictures. It has the disadvantage that most creatures present a rather strange appearance under infra-red because the colouring of skin, eyes, and hair appears quite different from that to which we are accustomed.

The noise made by the camera can be a problem, particularly if it has an automatic transport mechanism. It can be muffled somewhat by enclosing the machinery in a box lined with sound-absorbing material. It is well to remember that the camera does not have to be near the lights. For example, lights could be set up around a salt lick and connected to a camera, with a long lens, located some distance away. The photographer could, if convenient, operate both from a third location.

Finding Subjects

Knowing where to look for birds and other animals is a study in itself. A good knowledge of the subject's habits will help, but experience is the most important factor. The facts given in field guides about habitat, food, and nesting sites will help. Game wardens, park rangers, and naturalists usually know where to look for wildlife within their domains.

The most remarkable example of bird finding that I know of is not likely to be useful to many readers, but it is interesting nevertheless. It concerns the Wandering Albatross (*Diomedea exulans*). This largest of all sea birds, with its 11-foot wingspread, is almost never seen on or near land. The species is dispersed over thousands of square miles of trackless ocean in the Southern Hemisphere, yet we know enough about its habits to be able, given a ship and a weather map, to find the bird in mid-ocean. We also know, now, why old-time sailors were so superstitious about it.

This is the albatross of Coleridge's *Rime of the Ancient Mariner*. It soars continually, riding on air currents, and often follows ships. Now we know that to find the winds on which it floats so effortlessly, the Wanderer stays near the edges of areas of low barometric pressure. Consequently, when one is sighted from a ship heavy weather is almost sure to follow.

Camera Traps

The camera trap is an arrangement by which the subject operates the camera, and usually the lights as well. These devices are dear to gadgeteers, of whom a great many are also interested in photography, or at least, in photographic equipment. It is easy to find published instructions for making a variety of traps, but it is hard to find a good picture that was taken by one.

Operating a camera trap is a kind of photographic roulette; one never knows what will turn up on the film. In fact, I have seen this mentioned, in all seriousness, as one of the chief attractions of this sort of work.

A simple trap using a non-automatic camera will take only one picture each time it is loaded. If the photographer sets it every day it may be months before he will get one picture.

Primitive traps, like early remote-control arrangements, use a thread to trip the shutter. The thread is strung across a game trail or attached to a piece of bait. It is essential that the thread be strong enough to operate the shutter but not strong enough to drag the camera if the subject should decide to make off with the bait. The usual trap can be set off by a falling acorn or even a strong wind. If an animal does operate it, the picture may show just the tip of his tail as he leaves the scene. I have also seen pictures of skunks and woodchucks trying to squeeze under the trip cord. They look just as uncomfortable as tourists doing the limbo. But the biggest problem in camera traps is to get the species one wants and not something else. If the camera is set at the right height and distance for a moose, it will not take a good picture of a mouse.

A higher yield—in quantity if not in quality—can be expected from an automatic camera. The arrangement is similar to a remote-control one except that some tripping device is added. This can be any gadget that will complete an electrical connection when the subject is in the right place. There are micro switches sensitive enough to be operated by a bird landing on a branch. There are also electronic relays capable of being activated by almost any stimulus one could name. The familiar 'electric eye' operates when a beam of light is interrupted. A similar cell can be used with an invisible beam. A relay can also be made to respond to a sound or even to the change in capacitance caused by an object passing near a concealed metal plate.

All such devices have the same disadvantage: they are too easily triggered by unknown occurrences, falling leaves, insects, or animals of the wrong kind. Whatever control the photographer has over the content of his picture is exercised by his skill in placing and adjusting the tripping devices so that only the desired subject will operate them.

It is imperative that any mechanically-driven camera used in such a set-up has a switch or clutch that will turn off or disengage the drive mechanism when the end of the film is reached. Sooner or later some subject will stand on the switch or some accidental stimulus will turn the motor on and leave it on until the power supply is exhausted. If the camera does not have a cut-off switch or clutch, the film will be torn to shreds.

There is some doubt, I think, whether camera trapping should be considered part of photography at all, and whether the man or the machine should get credit for the results. The element of skill is so minor and the element of chance so overwhelming, that I think it should be classified as a game. It is comforting to note, however, that judging by the results that have been published, the live photographer is in no danger of being made obsolete by the trap.

13:

Handling Subjects

THE most exasperating words to a photographer are, 'What a beautiful picture! You must have a very expensive camera.'

There is a universal tendency—encouraged, of course, by advertising—to over-rate the mechanical and under-rate the human contributions to any worthwhile endeavour. We would like to believe that if we bought the kind of camera some well-known expert uses, we could take the same pictures he does. This is only one step removed from the educational message of television—that if we smoke the right cigarette beautiful girls will attend us at every turn.

Books like this one inevitably contribute to the deception by presenting detailed information on the mechanical aspects of photography, while passing over the more important mental aspects with no more than a few generalities. It should be sobering to remember that good—even great—nature photographs were taken before the development of modern photographic materials and equipment. Obviously, the fanciest machinery will not enable anyone to photograph an animal unless he can first find the animal and manoeuvre his camera into range.

Skill in handling subjects is one of those complex abilities that seem to be a blend of experience, attitude, and knack. It is, therefore, very hard to teach. The most important lesson for any nature photographer is to study his subjects and learn from them. The suggestions that follow can do no more than speed up that process a bit.

Timing

In Chapter 7 we mentioned briefly the characteristic movement of a flower and how it should be studied to find the moment of rest when the flower would be still long enough to have its picture taken. Other things have characteristic patterns of movement too—waves, insects, animals, and even people. One of the skills that a photographer must develop is the ability to sense these patterns and move with them, so that he can have his shutter open at the right moment. Many kinds of technical photography (discussed briefly in the next chapter) depend upon similar timing, but done at higher speeds by electronic devices.

The role of timing is probably most apparent in sports pictures. We have all seen pictures of a high-jumper clearing the bar, and if we have thought about it we know that there is an instant when he is relatively motionless, just as he reaches maximum height and before he starts down. This instant is shorter than the time it takes for the photographer to make up his mind and push the shutter release, so he must learn to start pushing the button just before the peak is reached. The photographer's ability to anticipate action is much more important than the speeds of which his film, shutter, or flash units may be capable, because the problem is not simply to get a sharp image but rather to catch the action at the instant that makes the best picture. Usually the moment of peak action combines maximum pictorial effectiveness with minimum motion, but not always, and careful observation will sometimes reveal that the peak moment does not occur when you would expect it. Gjon Mili, the engineer-turned-photographer who pioneered the use of electronic flash, discovered when he was assigned to photograph basketball that the most exciting moment in the game came not when the winning basket was made, but rather when a basket was *missed* and both teams tried to get the ball on the rebound. In some of his most dramatic basketball pictures the ball was not on its way up to the basket, but down from the backboard. This is a good illustration of the need for studying the subject itself, rather than using what seems beforehand to be the obvious moment to shoot.

It is perhaps less apparent that a similar sense of timing is required for most pictures of people. One of the things that makes bad snapshots bad is that the subject is asked to hold still for so long that his expression 'freezes'. The best pictures of people are taken at the natural peak moments while they are conversing or doing something. The photographs of public figures, on which our images of them are largely based, involve the same element. Press photographers, or at least the better ones, know that everyone has characteristic gestures, expressions, and ways of moving. After watching famous public figures for a few minutes, an experienced photographer can anticipate each expression. (And incidentally, public figures who want to make an impression on people must learn to give press photographers opportunities to get animated pictures of them. When Khrushchev banged his shoe on the table at the United Nations, he was careful to first shout and wave so that the photographers would have time to focus their cameras on him.)

When an Eskimo goes hunting seals at the *sina* (the edge of the ice) in the spring he hides behind a white cloth shield and creeps up on a seal that is basking on the ice. The Eskimo knows that every few minutes the seal will raise its head and look around. At those times the Eskimo hides behind his shield or pretends to be another seal. When the seal dozes again, the Eskimo creeps closer. Often he must get close enough to hit the seal with a harpoon, because if he used a rifle the seal would roll into the water and sink.

A similar technique is used by experienced nature photographers. They know, for example, that most animals when grazing or feeding raise their heads periodically to look around. The photographer has only to focus on the animal and wait.

A caterpillar or lizard if placed on a short branch will usually crawl to the end of the branch and then pause while deciding what to do next. The photographer can focus on the end of the branch and be reasonably sure that his subject will hold still at that spot. A little study will show whether the particular species prefers to crawl up or down, toward the light or away from it.

Turtles and other reptiles like to warm themselves in the sun, and when basking will hold still for long periods. They and their close relatives, the amphibians, are quite sensitive to temperature. Laboratory specimens or captive subjects can be made sluggish and tractable by cooling them in a refrigerator. They will slowly return to normal activity as they warm up, thus allowing the photographer to set up his equipment and take his picture at the desired moment. Turtles that stubbornly hide in their shells can be encouraged to emerge by placing them briefly in the sun or under a floodlight.

Nocturnal Searches

One of the best ways to find many kinds of creatures is to go look-ing at night with a light. This technique is so effective for deer that its use in hunting is universally prohibited. Many smaller creatures can be spotted by the reflection of the light in their eyes. Some will stare at the light as though hypnotized. The light can be used to locate the subject and focus on it, and the picture can then be made with flash. At least two flash units are normally required to give 'rounded' lighting, requiring two people to carry and aim them. Night pictures are seldom as satisfactory as ones made in day-light, but for nocturnal subjects they are, of course, truer to life.

Night is the best time to look for marine subjects near the shore. Exploring a few tide pools with a light and dip net will usually yield subjects enough for a full day's shooting. Night is also the time to look for frogs, toads, and other amphibians, and many fresh-water creatures. A great convenience is a 'headlight' of the type worn by miners, that leaves the hands free. There is also a large waterproof electric lantern that can be used underwater as well as in air.

Whose Eye Level?

It is usually best to photograph animals from about their own eye level. When other angles are used, it should be for a definite reason. For example, if there are distinctive markings on the animal's back it may be best to photograph it from above. If, on the other hand, the predatory nature of some animal such as the praying mantis is to be accentuated, then a victim's-eye view, emphasizing the jaws, mandibles, and spine-covered forearms, may be the most appro-priate. Most photographers are reluctant to unbend and bring themselves down to the subject's level. They fail to use the most effective viewpoints for some pictures, and unnecessarily restrict their photographic vocabulary. Consider for a moment how pictures of people would look if all of them were taken from overhead!

The Camouflaged Subject

Subjects that are comouflaged for their own protection pose special problems for the photographer. The first problem is to find them, the next is to figure out how to photograph them without either falsifying their natural situation or permitting them to disappear in the picture. It must be remembered that camouflaged subjects will normally be *less* visible in a photograph than in life because the camera has only one eye and lacks the highly sophisticated visual mechanism that aids us in perceiving shapes.

No one wants to photograph a nature subject against an alien background, but on the other hand the photograph will not be very useful if the subject cannot be seen in it. It is possible to differentiate the subject from the background by using special photographic techniques, such as a monochromatic light source or a film and filter combination sensitive only to some wavelength to which the subject and background respond differently. This is the technique used in military reconnaissance. Before the days of aerial photography, armies used colour-blind observers for the same purpose. But in most nature photographs our aim is to show the subject as it appears to a normal observer, only more clearly. These special techniques will not help toward that end because neither subject nor background will be shown in the photograph as it appears to the eye. Ways must be found to differentiate the subject by more natural means. Usually it is the choice of viewpoint that provides the answer.

A low viewpoint may make it possible to show the subject against the sky or to get it far enough in front of the surroundings to stand out. Here again, backlighting is very helpful. The use of a large aperture may throw the background out of focus and differentiate it that way. It may be helpful to make the background lighter or darker by reflecting light into it or throwing a shadow on it. The choice would depend on whether the subject is light or dark.

Marine Subjects

Camouflage is a particular problem with some marine subjects, and is mentioned briefly in Chapter 11. Because of this and other problems of the underwater environment, small marine animals are usually best photographed in an aquarium. The camera can be outside, unencumbered by a watertight housing, the lighting can be controlled, and the subject can be discouraged from swimming away. Most important, the camera can easily be placed at or below the subject's own level, if that is the best viewpoint.

The ordinary little aquariums sold by scientific supply houses are convenient and inexpensive. A fancier type can be made, having a trapezoidal floor plan so that the back panel is wider than the front. This is useful because the camera takes in a wider field of view in the background than in the foreground, and with a

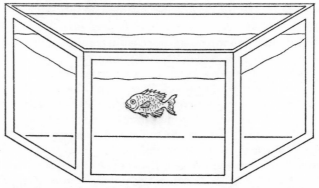

Fig. 24 Trapezoidal aquarium places rear corners outside the picture area.

rectangular aquarium only a small section in the centre can be used. Otherwise the back corners will appear in the picture.

Among the indispensable accessories for aquarium work are several sheets of glass that can be used as partitions to confine the subject in the right part of the tank. Backgrounds are usually placed behind the tank and may be sheets of cardboard, pieces of cloth, or even a blue sky. Occasionally a piece of coral or some other natural stage prop is used in the background. With small subjects, however, the background is likely to be so far out of focus that anything placed there will not be seen. The biggest problem is coping with reflections on all the various glass surfaces. Often these reflections are not noticed until they show up in the final print or transparency. Particularly troublesome are shiny metal parts on the camera and white shirts worn by the photographer and his helpers. It is helpful to pin a black cloth into a hood, enclosing the front of the camera and the front surface of the aquarium. This does not cure reflections on the back of the aquarium, but they are less troublesome. It cuts off some of the light on the subject, and for that reason may not always be feasible. The important thing is for the photographer to develop an awareness of these reflections, and for him always to study the image *with the lens stopped down* to the aperture that will be used for the picture. This is not possible with a range-finder or twin-lens camera, which is a good reason for not using those types of cameras with aquariums.

It should hardly be necessary to mention that animals in aquariums must be provided with air to breathe. The air dissolved in water freshly scooped from a lake or stream or from the sea will be sufficient for a few hours, but if specimens are to be kept longer they must be provided either with frequent changes of water or a supply of air. Incidentally, tap water should not be used in aquariums unless you are sure it has not been disinfected with chlorine, sent through copper pipes, or otherwise rendered poisonous to aquatic life.

An aquarium aerator is a useful gadget for anyone who is going to keep specimens, even for a short time. For field use, there are low-voltage models that will operate on dry batteries or from the battery of a car. Specimens can also be kept in a fisherman's bait bucket or some other container through which water can circulate. There is a danger, though, that some ingenious predator may be able to open the bucket and help himself to a free meal. Once upon a time my wife and I captured an evil-looking moray eel in the shallows off a coral island where we had established a field camp. We wanted to photograph it, but we had promised to go somewhere else that morning, so we left the moray coiled in a bucket of sea water and put the bucket in a safe place where it would be shaded from the sun. When we came back, the eel was gone. Only later did we discover that someone had once abandoned a couple of cats on the island. Apparently it was they or their offspring who absconded with the eel.

The same sort of aquarium, without water, is a convenient enclosure for all sorts of small specimens. The glass sides keep the subject in camera range without interfering too much with the light and the camera's view. A closely fitted cover of screening is a useful accessory.

Safeguarding Subjects

The story of the missing eel serves also to point up another problem. No photographer wants to endanger the lives of his subjects by thoughtless acts, but sometimes it requires a thorough knowledge of the ecology to appreciate the effects of what we do. If we pull back branches to expose a bird's nest for a photograph, we may also expose the nest to predators. The sunlight that we admit by tying back branches may be hot enough to kill unprotected eggs or baby birds, and the mere presence of the photographer may keep the parents away long enough to doom their young.

When it comes to safeguarding subjects, most of us draw the line somewhere. We suffer no pangs of conscience when we kill the germs that live on our teeth or the mosquitoes that wander into our tents. Few would go as far as the famous photomicrographer Dr. Roman Vishniac does, and return algae to the same spot from which they were collected. I am even inclined to feel that my wife went a bit too far when she shepherded a Portuguese man-of-war we had been photographing out into the current to prevent it from being washed ashore and got a painful sting for her trouble. But no one who comes to know and understand wild things is likely to harm them intentionally. It is our lack of knowledge that sometimes endangers them; our best intentions sometimes bring bad results.

Feeding animals is a good way to gain their confidence and attract them to your lens, but any sustained programme of feeding creates dangers for the subject. No such programme should be started without a clear understanding of its probable effects.

If a feeding station is established for birds, it must be made cat-proof and so placed that it cannot be turned into a baited trap. If the hand-outs induce birds to remain in the vicinity after their normal migration time, the feeding must be continued throughout the winter. Otherwise birds that would ordinarily have gone south may starve.

It is not a good idea in any case to encourage wild animals to become dependent on hand-outs from humans, as the perennial problems with bears in Yellowstone Park demonstrate. The operators of resort concessions in the park formerly fed their garbage to the bears as the simplest way of getting rid of it. This

[25] *An example of photography as a tool of science. Taken with high-speed electronic flash actuated when the bird interrupts a beam of light, this picture is part of a series used to study how canaries land on a perch. (See page 160, dealing with the safeguarding of subjects.)*

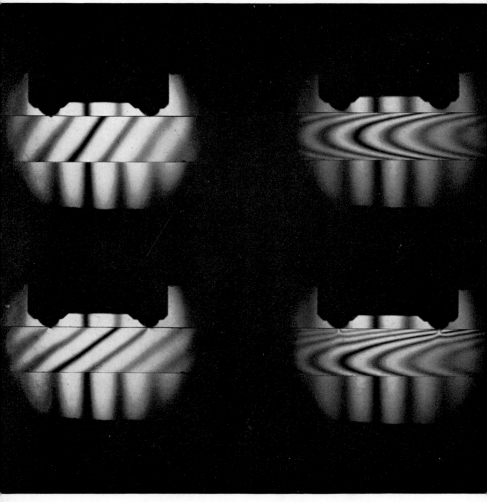

[26] *Science photography without a camera. Film exposed directly in a polarimeter shows effects of strain in tempered and untempered glass. Tempered glass (right) will stand greater strain. (See page 169.)*

encouraged the bears to give up hunting and hang around the picnic grounds, where the damage was compounded by a diet of sandwiches and candy bars. There is now an entire lost generation of bears that have never learned to find their own food. Harried park officials have their hands full trying to re-educate both the bears and the people.

The white-tailed deer common in the Eastern U.S.A. present a more complicated problem. These animals are more numerous now than they were before America was colonized by Europeans. The elimination of predators and competitors for the food supply, coupled with the dwindling forest area, has produced a population larger than the environment can support. Thus the photographer who wants to attract deer faces an unpleasant dilemma. If he feeds them they will lose some of their caution and may fall easy prey to hunters; if he does not feed them they may starve.

There is no satisfactory universal answer to these problems. All that can be said is that anyone who feeds wildlife should be sure that he knows what he is doing and is equipped to finish whatever programme he starts. It should not be necessary to mention that the food must be something the animal can digest, and that all wild animals should be treated with respect. Children should not try to feed animals from their hands. Even the tamest animals may kick or bite by accident.

Safeguarding the Photographer

There are times when protecting the photographer is as important as protecting the subject. Once in Antarctica when I was photographing a leopard seal stalking penguins, the seal suddenly rose out of the water a few feet in front of my lens, and seemed about to come up on the ice after me. I started to retreat, but slipped and fell. The seal did not seize his advantage, but I am inclined to feel that with such a subject the photographer should have a companion with a rifle just as insurance.

Few animals will go out of their way to molest humans, unless we consider mosquitoes, ticks, and the like, but commonsense precautions should never be omitted. Never go near baby animals; the mother may defend them. Never try to take food away from an animal. Be wary of large animals in the rutting season. Do not reach into holes or up on to ledges if you cannot see where you are reaching; you do not known what you may accidentally grab. Be sensible and you will be safe.

In this connection, a word about snakes may be in order. Snakes have played an important part in magic and mythology from earliest times. The lurking belief in magic is barely concealed in the irrational fear of snakes that some people have and in the many old wives' tales about them. More than a little of it is hidden in the frequently published advice that everyone going into the woods should carry a snake-bite kit or a supply of antivenom serum or wear leggings reinforced with wire screening, or heaven knows what other amulets. We would consider anyone rather odd who carried a pair of crutches on a trip as a precaution, but the chances of being bitten by a poisonous snake are much less than those of breaking a leg, and the number of injuries caused by attempts to treat snake bite exceeds those caused by actual bites. Antivenom serum should be administered only by a physician, and only after tests have shown that the patient is not allergic to it. Methods of first-aid treatment for snake bite are undergoing considerable study at the moment, and it is probable that the old standard advice will be revised, as has the advice concerning artificial respiration. With a little commonsense one can safely photograph poisonous snakes, but it would be wise to start with non-venomous ones.

With most live subjects, it is a great help to have an assistant who can concentrate on the subject, freeing the photographer to attend to his photographic problems. The assistant's job is to herd the subject into the right area and keep an eye on it while the photographer prepares and takes his pictures. My wife is a talented handler of animals and the ideal companion for a field trip. Once we caught an octopus in shallow water in the daytime and were able to get a series of pictures of it. The octopus is a very shy nocturnal animal and changes colour when upset. This one was very upset and tried to hide by digging a hole for itself under a rock. The handler's job in this case was to pull the animal out before it got too well dug in and then to keep it from escaping into deep water until the photography was done.

Indeed, the photographer's helper is the unsung hero of nature photography. Many of the impressive pictures that we see published would have been impossible for the photographer alone. Often they represent the fruits of collaboration between a photographer with expert knowledge of the medium and a scientist with expert knowledge of the subject.

This brings us back to the point with which this chapter—and indeed this book—began: It is the man who makes the picture, not the machine. All the cameras, lenses, film, filters, and techniques are less important than the ability to study living things and learn from them.

14:

Photography in Science

IN the natural history museums of the future, files of photographs and rolls of microfilm will be as important as the trays of 'study skins', jars of pickled specimens, and boxes of rocks that fill the basements and back rooms of such museums today.

A museum is like an iceberg in that at least nine tenths of it is out of sight. The exhibits seen by the public are only a small part of any museum's collections; the larger and more important parts are the reference collections used by the museum staff and other qualified scientists. It is such reference collections, for example, that are the basis for determining whether a newly discovered fish will be considered a new species or merely a variant of a known one. If it is a new species the discoverer may earn a bit of immortality by having his surname attached to its scientific name.

The value of these study collections will be greatly enhanced when adequately planned and competently executed photography becomes a regular part of them. Photography can record things too big to be collected, too fragile to be preserved, or too fleeting to be captured. It can record colours and textures that will not survive in a preserved specimen, and it can open new fields in which collecting has so far been impossible (e.g., a complete record of dances or rituals). It can be of even greater importance in communicating the results of natural science study to an ever-widening audience, no longer limited to those who can visit the museum in person.

In utilizing photography both for recording and for communication, natural science is at present far behind such fields as nuclear physics or aerodynamics. It is still traditional in field expeditions for the most junior scientist or graduate student to be given the job of operating the camera, and it is still common for expeditions to set out for remote parts of the world carrying photographic equipment that no one in the party has ever used or even tested. It is not surprising that photographs made under such conditions so often fail to contribute to the results.

In this chapter, some of the ways that photography is used in science are briefly discussed.

Photography Without Light

The radiation visible to humans, called light, is only a small part of a continuous spectrum of electro-magnetic waves that also includes, on one side, radio and heat waves, and on the other, X-rays and gamma rays. All these waves are of the same nature and travel at the same speed (roughly 186,000 miles per second in a vacuum). They differ only in wavelength, and this difference is responsible for their widely different properties.

Photographic materials can be made to respond to wavelengths well outside the narrow sensitivity of the eye. X-ray photographs are the most common example of this. Gamma rays are used to make similar 'shadowgraphs' of metal objects.

The wavelengths close to those of light have properties that are similar to light. Ultra-violet affects films the way light does, and eliminating it is a problem in landscape and snow photography. Infra-red, on the other end of the visible spectrum, is most useful for penetrating atmospheric haze in long distance and aerial photography. These forms of radiation also have other, more technical uses.

Photography by Ultra-violet

Ultra-violet causes many materials to fluoresce, that is, to give off light by converting some of the ultra-violet energy to a different wavelength. This is the mechanism by which light is produced in fluorescent lamps. 'Daylight fluorescent' paints and dyes fluoresce so strongly that even the comparatively weak ultra-violet present in daylight will make them give off enough light to be visible in spite of the surrounding daylight. Such materials appear much brighter on cloudy days, when the visible part of the daylight is less bright but the ultra-violet is still strong. Fluorescent materials are the only substances that apparently reflect more light than falls on them. It follows that measurements of incident light will not give accurate exposure information for them.

There are two ways of photographing by ultra-violet. One is to use the ultra-violet as a 'light' source and photograph the reflection of it by the subject, a process exactly like ordinary photography except that ultra-violet is used instead of light. Since all photographic films are sensitive to ultra-violet as well as to whatever wavelengths of light they may be designed to use, special films are not ordinarily required for this work. However, so many common objects exhibit fluorescence (including the photographer's teeth, eyes, and fingernails and the starch in his shirt) that it is usually necessary to use filters to exclude the light produced by fluorescence when the photograph is to be made by ultra-violet alone. It is impossible, of course, for the photographer to see what his camera is going to record, since our eyes are not sensitive to ultra-violet. Whatever image the photographer may see is produced by light—either from fluorescence or from imperfect filtering of the ultra-violet sources.

Photography by reflected ultra-violet is used for differentiating areas that may look the same but reflect ultra-violet to different degrees. A common application is in the detection of forged paintings and documents. (Fluorescence photography is also used in these studies.) Reflected and transmitted ultra-violet is also used in photomicrography, where its short wavelength permits greater resolution than is possible with light.

The second, and much more common, use of ultra-violet is as a source of energy for the production of light by fluorescence—light which can then be photographed like any other light, in black-and-white or in colour. The only difference between this and conventional photography is that the ultra-violet must be prevented by filters from reaching the film so that it will not 'wash out' the image.

Fluorescence photography is widely used in the study of minerals (many of which fluoresce in brilliant colour), for recording paper chromatographs, in photomicrography of materials that fluoresce naturally and of those that can be differentiated by means of fluorescent stains, and in numerous other fields.

Ultra-violet includes a considerable range of wavelengths, from 400 millimicrons (mμ) downward. The region near the visible spectrum is the most useful for photography. Below about 350 mμ, glass lenses cannot be used because they are opaque to these wavelengths and, in addition, they may fluoresce. Naturally, these limitations do not apply in fluorescence photography since in that case the photograph is not being made by the ultra-violet but by light, and the ultra-violet is prevented by a filter from reaching the lens. Short wavelength ultra-violet (below 350 mμ) is irritating to the eyes, and may cause the eyeballs to fluoresce so strongly that everything is seen through a luminous haze. Protective goggles must therefore be worn. Long wavelength or 'near' ultra-violet does not cause such problems.

Because common ultra-violet sources, such as mercury vapour lamps, emit specific narrow bands of wavelengths (called 'lines') they are sometimes used like monochromatic light sources, described later in this chapter.

Infra-red Photography

In Chapter 5 we discussed the use of infra-red instead of light for photographing distant landscapes through haze, probably the commonest application of infra-red photography. In aerial photography, particularly for military purposes, the use of infra-red has been developed to an astonishing degree. Not only is it possible to photograph terrain through clouds from an aircraft that is therefore invisible from the ground, but it is even possible to detect events that occurred before the photograph was made. Where an object, such as a truck or missile, casts a shadow and thus prevents the ground from absorbing infra-red radiation, the pattern of the shadow will remain for as long as twenty-four hours and can be detected in an infra-red photograph by a skilled photo interpreter.

Aerial photographs made by infra-red will differentiate many objects that appear the same to the eye or to an ordinary film. For example, foresters use such photographs to determine the proportions of various kinds of trees in large wooded areas. Terrestrial infra-red photography is used in so many fields of science that it is impossible to list them all here, and astronomical photography by infra-red has revealed thousands of formerly unknown invisible stars.

In ultra-violet photography, ordinary films are used with special light sources. In infra-red the opposite is true. Sunlight, incandescent lamps and flash bulbs all emit quantities of infra-red. The only common light sources that do not are fluorescent lamps. But ordinary films are not sensitive to infra-red, so special films must be used. Some special precautions, explained in the handbooks (see Bibliography), must be observed in handling them as not all substances that are opaque to light are opaque to infra-red. Infra-red-sensitive films are sensitive also to blue, so filters are ordinarily necessary to prevent light from reaching the film.

Focus for Ultra-violet and Infra-red

Lenses form an image by bending the light rays, but the extent to which a ray is bent depends on its wavelength. It is this fact that causes a prism to separate the component colours of white light. With a rudimentary lens (like a magnifying glass) the images of different colours will be in slightly different planes. The blue image is closest to the lens and the red one farthest from it, with the rest of the spectrum in between. (This is why the layers of colour film are arranged in that order.) This slight discrepancy is called chromatic aberration. Photographic lenses are corrected so as to reduce their chromatic aberration to a negligible amount within the visible spectrum. When wavelengths outside that range are used, the image may not be in focus at the same place as it is with light. In the 'near' portion of the ultra-violet, for which glass lenses are suitable, the difference is slight and is usually taken care of by using a small aperture. With infra-red, a correction in focus is usually necessary.

Many lenses have a focusing mark for infra-red on the mount. Usually it is engraved in red, and sometimes the letter R is used. If the lens is focused visually, the focus can be corrected for infra-red by moving the lens so that the distance which then appeared opposite the focusing mark will fall opposite the red mark. The correction will ordinarily increase the lens-to-film distance by about one fourth of 1 per cent of the focal length. Because ordinary lenses have various aberrations that are corrected for light but not for other wavelengths, the smallest practical aperture should always be used.

Monochromatic Light Sources

Because of the slight difference in focus of different wavelengths, higher resolution can be achieved with a single wavelength or narrow band than with a wide band such as the whole visible spectrum. For some extremely demanding work, a monochromatic light source will give a sharper image than ordinary light. The most common such sources are sodium vapour lamps, such as those used on highways. They produce a lot of light, and 95 per cent of it is at one wavelength—589 mμ. The remaining 5 per cent can, if necessary, be screened out by filters.

Mercury vapour lamps (also used for highway lighting) supply three 'lines'—546 mμ, which is green, 436 mμ, which is blue, and 365 mμ, which is ultra-violet. These wavelengths can be isolated with filters.

Monochromatic light is useful chiefly for very small subjects photographed with considerable magnification. It is also used to differentiate colours that might be indistinguishable under white light. In photomicrography, both monochromatic light and monochromatic ultra-violet are useful. Since the resolving power of the microscope objective is a limiting factor, and since it depends on wavelength, highest resolution is obtained with a source such as the 365 mμ line of mercury vapour. Shorter wavelengths can be used, but they are not as easy to obtain because they will not pass through glass and are consequently difficult to control. For wavelengths below 310 mμ, not only the lamp but also the microscope lenses must be made of quartz.

Polarized Light

Polarized light is another special type of illumination, although it looks like ordinary light to us. Some substances, notably crystals, alter the polarity of light passing through them. This property is used to distinguish them in photographs, usually made with a microscope. A polarizer is placed in the path of the illuminating light and another is placed in the path of the image, usually in the microscope eyepiece. If the two polarizers are at right angles all the direct light passed by the first one will be rejected by the second, and only the light whose polarity has been altered by the specimen will be passed. In practice, the eyepiece polarizer is rotated until the angle giving maximum clarity is found. This technique is useful in the study of minerals and of snow and ice.

Polarized light is used in engineering to make stress visible. The stresses that will be developed in a bridge can be studied in advance if a model of the structure is made in transparent plastic. Under polarized light the lines of stress will appear as purple and green lines when the model is subjected to mechanical stress. The same technique can be used with objects that are naturally transparent, such as samples of glass. Stress that has been applied in forming the glass will be 'frozen in' when the glass cools (see Plate 26).

The use of polarized light was mentioned in Chapter 5. Light that has been polarized by placing polarizing filters over the light sources can be controlled by another polarizer over the lens, and is most useful for photographing non-metallic objects that exhibit objectionable surface reflections (pieces of glazed pottery, for example). At certain angles the reflections can be almost completely eliminated. This is the best technique for photographing specimens that are under glass or sealed in transparent plastic. A lesser degree of control can be obtained by using a polarizer over the lens alone.

Microscope Photography

Photomicrography is a subject for a separate book; a brief outline is all that can be included here. The camera is the least important part of the equipment since its only function is to hold the film. The image is formed by the lenses of the microscope. Whether the subject will be distinguishable from its surroundings is largely a matter of lighting.

Photographs of microscope images can be made with simple cameras in the following way: the camera lens is set at infinity, and the camera is mounted so that the centre of the front surface of the lens is at the eyepoint of the microscope ocular. The eyepoint is the point where the light from the microscope forms the smallest dot, and can be found by holding a piece of paper over the microscope ocular and moving it up and down. Exposure is best found by trial. The camera aperture must be wide open, as it is not at the right place in the system to control the amount of light reaching the film, so exposure time is the only controllable factor.

It is never desirable to have unnecessary lens elements in any optical system, so a better technique is to use a camera from which the lens can be removed and rely on the microscope optics to form the image on the film. The camera shutter can be used, but a focal-plane shutter is likely to cause vibration and consequent unsharpness. A leaf shutter is better in this regard, but it must be located at or near the eyepoint to give uniform exposure throughout the field. (This location is analogous to that of the ordinary leaf shutter between the elements of a lens.) It is not necessary to use a shutter if the exposure can be controlled by turning the light on and off. Such a system eliminates the danger of vibration from the shutter, and also from the mirror in a reflex camera or reflex-focusing accessory. A shutter may be used to keep light from reaching the film during preliminary setting up. Then when every-thing is ready, the light is turned off, the shutter is opened, and the light is turned on (either manually or by a timer) for the exposure. After the exposure the light is turned off and the shutter closed again.

It is possible to remove the camera from the microscope and set up the subject by looking through the eyepiece in the ordinary way, but this leaves some uncertainty as to whether the photo-graphed image will be in focus. It is better to use a device that will permit examination of the image while the camera is in place. The single-lens reflex type of camera and the view camera with its ground-glass screen do this without accessories, requiring only a coupling device to attach them to the microscope. Other cameras, like the range-finder types, have microscope adaptors that provide either reflex focusing or a 'beam splitter', which is a non-moving half-silvered mirror that deflects part of the beam to an eyepiece while permitting the rest of it to pass through to the film. Since the beam splitter does not move, it does not introduce any vibra-tion, and the reduction in the intensity of the image caused by deflecting part of the light is not usually important. If the subject is stationary, the exposure can be as long as necessary. If it is moving, continuous viewing is necessary to keep it in focus and in view.

The resolution of a photographed microscope image is limited by the objective lens and the wavelength of the illumination. The photographic set-up has little effect on it. For a particular lens and wavelength, the limit of usable magnification can be calculated. Beyond that limit, the image can be made larger but no additional detail can be resolved. This is called 'empty magnification'. The image on the film is usually smaller than the maximum. It can then be enlarged photographically up to the maximum before empty magnification occurs. Enlargements beyond the theoretical maximum are used, of course, where they must be viewed from a greater than normal distance, as in museum displays or slides to be projected for an audience.

Exposure for Photomicrography

Only very specialized meters are capable of measuring the intensity of the light transmitted through a microscope, so in most cases exposure is based on trial and error. Once a standard exposure has been determined for a particular microscope, light, film, and magnification, exposure for other combinations may be derived from it. With large-size cameras, Polaroid film provides a quick way of making test exposures. A special Polaroid camera is available for microscope work.

Lighting for Photomicrography

Lighting is of great importance because photomicrographs do not have the appearance of 'depth' that ordinary photographs have. The use of stains was once the only way of making transparent subjects visible and differentiating one from another. Now a number of more sophisticated optical techniques have extended the usefulness of the microscope. Basically, these are all advanced methods of lighting. Ultra-violet and infra-red are used with microscopes as they are with larger subjects. They rely on photography to make the results visible. Fluorescence photography uses ultra-violet to stimulate the production of light by fluorescent substances. The use of polarized and monochromatic light has been mentioned above. In addition, dark-field illumination, phase contrast, and interference microscopy, which are all special ways of controlling the light that passes through and around the specimen, have made it possible to see and photograph many previously invisible subjects.

Special Purpose Films

It is possible to control the sensitivity of photographic apparatus over a very wide range, and thus add new dimensions to what can be seen. Astronomy, for example, is no longer limited to the study of stars that can be seen by an observer at the telescope; thousands of additional stars have been discovered in photographs because the photographic plate is capable of adding together all the tiny quantities of light emitted by the star over a period of hours. (A precise drive mechanism is used to keep the telescope aimed at the same point in the sky while the earth turns.) Films sensitive to infra-red have recorded other stars that are invisible to the eye. The latest developments go beyond photography, using radio waves emitted by the stars.

The ability of a film to add together small increments of light is the basis of all time exposures. The sensitivity of the process can be controlled so as to record desired images and reject others. For example, photographers routinely photograph the displays in store windows at night, using long time exposures. People may walk back and forth in front of the window, and even stop to look at it, but they are invisible to the film because they are present for only a fraction of the total exposure time. At the other end of the scale, films can record an image in a much shorter time than the eye, enabling the film to 'see' events that are invisible to us.

The photographer has at his disposal an enormous variety of films, many of them having remarkable characteristics. There are thin-base films of extremely high resolving power and there are films of enormous speed. There are also films with special contrast characteristics. For example, one special film increases the separation between highlight tones without adding contrast to the shadows. It was designed for copying photographs, but has many other uses. Fine Grain Positive, despite its name, is not a reversal film but one designed for making positive transparencies (slides) from negatives. It has a 'colour-blind' emulsion sensitive only to blue and capable of very high resolution. Lithographic films and high-contrast films of the type used for microfilm recording convert all tones of grey into either black or white. By careful choice of exposure they can be made to discriminate details that are hard to see. Many more specialized films with unusual characteristics are made for technical, aerial, and graphic arts applications. Often they have other uses, sometimes unforeseen, for the science photographer.

Photography Conquers Time

The most important uses of photography in science result from the photographer's ability to control time. Our knowledge of lightning is augmented because we can capture the flash on film and study it at leisure. Such studies as those on how a frog jumps (reported in *Natural History* magazine) would be impossible without photography done with high-speed repetitive flash. The famous photographs of running water and of drops of milk falling into a saucer of milk, made by Harold Edgerton, have shown us that high-speed photography is more than a means of ensuring a sharp picture of a moving object; it reveals events and processes previously invisible because they occur so fast.

With a precisely controlled interval between exposures—whether they be superimposed on one film or recorded on separate frames of film—the photograph becomes a device for measuring the distance travelled by a moving object in a known time, and hence its speed. Moving subjects can be studied with a series of high-speed photographs 'played back' at reduced speed—a sophisticated version of the 'slow motion' that seems so comic in home movies. This high-speed cinematography is much used in rocketry and other branches of engineering. Its effect is to 'stretch' or amplify time. The opposite effect is achieved in time-lapse photography, in which a sequence of images is 'played back' faster than it was recorded. Gradual developments, such as the growth of plants or the erosion of sand dunes, can be seen in motion by this technique.

The limit of speed obtainable with mechanical shutters is from 1/800 to 1/1000 sec. depending upon size and design. Very much higher speeds are obtained in cinematography by using moving mirrors instead. In still photography, high speeds are ordinarily obtained by using light sources of short duration. Since the film is usually uncovered before and after the flash, the work must be done in darkness, or at least in light very much less intense than that used to take the picture.

Coherent Light

Recent developments in light sources may open possibilities for photography that we cannot yet conceive of. Optical masers (or lasers) generate light that is far more monochromatic than that from any other source and, in addition, is coherent, which means that all the waves vibrate together. A beam of such light shows very little 'spread'. In fact, scientists at the Massachussetts Institute of Technology have used a laser to throw a spot two miles wide on the face of the moon. The intensity of light produced by lasers has reached more than 5,000 million times the intensity of the noonday sun. The applications of coherent light to photography are as yet unknown.

Photography in Archaeology

An illustration of what photography can do in science is provided by present-day archaeology. By a fortuitous accident, archaeology has benefited from the thousands upon thousands of aerial photographs made for mapping, surveying, prospecting, military reconnaissance, and many other uses. It turns out that aerial photographs are the quickest means of locating probable archaeological sites, and often show features that are not visible from the ground. The Indian mounds built about 400 B.C. at Poverty Point, Louisiana, were discovered by Dr. James A. Ford of The American Museum of Natural History from a study of survey photographs in the files of the Mississippi River Commission.

Because of photography there is now a back-log of known and suspected sites waiting to be investigated. Photography will also reduce, sometimes by years, the time required to map and excavate them. In a short time (in archaeological terms) photography has become so important in this field that no expedition would now be undertaken without providing for it.

Conclusion

The science photographer stands on the boundary between the known and the unknown. He is constantly called upon to photograph things that have never been photographed—and perhaps never seen before. There are technical problems to be solved, and he needs a thorough understanding of the medium, but the real problems are conceptual ones—figuring out what kind of picture will best reveal the significant aspects of the subject. This is the essential problem in all photography.

An Annotated Bibliography

This is not a complete bibliography on photography, or even on nature photography. It lists books about which I have some remarks to make, and ones that will probably be appreciated by readers who like this book enough to have read this far.

ON PHOTOGRAPHY IN GENERAL

DESCHIN, JACOB. *Say It With Your Camera; an Approach to Creative Photography* (McGraw-Hill, 1950). About photography as communication.

DESCHIN, JACOB. *35-mm. Photography* (San Francisco: Camera Craft, 1953). One of the few elementary books that pays adequate attention to the non-technical aspects of photography.

HORDER, ALAN (ed.). *The Ilford Manual of Photography* (Ilford Ltd. Revised and reissued periodically). In the preface to this solid 725-page work, Horder apologizes for not having had enough space to discuss colour photography.

WALLS, HENRY JAMES. *How Photography Works* (Focal Press, 1959). Not elementary as the title would suggest. A sound treatment, becoming quite advanced. Good discussion of psychological factors in seeing.

PHOTOGRAPHIC HANDBOOKS

By far the most accurate and readable information on photography, both fundamental and specialized, is in the series of data books issued by Kodak Limited at prices from 6s. to 15s. Several related data books sold as a unit in one binder constitute a handbook. All are revised periodically. I have seen expensive correspondence courses that did not contain as much information. The following titles are among those in the series likely to be useful for further reading on nature photography:

Fundamentals

Camera Technique for Professional Photographers (O-18) (Contains the best available exposition of how to use the view camera's swings and tilts, plus good basic optics.)

Adventures in Outdoor Colour Slides (E-9) (Elementary and very good.)

Materials

Kodak Films in Rolls for Black-and-White Photography (F-13)
Negative Making with Kodak Black-and-White Sheet Films (F-5)
Kodak Filters and Pola-Screens (B-1) (Elementary.)
Kodak Wratten Filters for Scientific and Technical Use (B-3) (Advanced.)

Processing

Enlarging in Black-and-White and Colour (G-16)
Professional Printing with Kodak Photographic Papers (G-5)
Processing Chemicals and Formulas (J-1)

Colour Photography

Colour as Seen and Photographed (E-74) (Basic and excellent.)
Colour Photography Outdoors (E-75)
Applied Colour Photography Indoors (E-76)
Kodak Colour Films (E-77)
Printing Colour Negatives (E-66)

Lighting

Flash Pictures (C-2)
Studio Lighting for Product Photography (O-16)

Photographing Small Objects

Photography of Gross Specimens (N-5) (Much more useful than the title would suggest. Written for pathologists with little background in photography, but lots in medicine.)
Copying (M-1) (Good for flat subjects.)
Studio Lighting for Product Photography (O-16) (Good for immobile subjects.)

Specialized Photography

Photography Through the Microscope (P-2)
Infra-red and Ultra-violet Photography (M-3)
Photomicrography of Metals (P-39) (Also applicable to other opaque subjects.)
Kodak Plates and Films for Science and Industry (P-9)

Pocket Data Guides

These are not books but spiral-bound collections of tables, computers, sample filters, etc.
Kodak Master Photoguide (R-21)
Kodak Colour Dataguide (R-19)

ON NATURE PHOTOGRAPHY

CRUICKSHANK, ALLAN D. (ed.) with Charles E. Mohr, Edward S. Ross, Herman W. Kitchen, and Rutherford Platt. *Hunting with the Camera; A Guide to Techniques and Adventure in the Field* (New York: Harper and Brothers, 1957). As is perhaps inevitable in a book with five authors, there is repetition and uneven quality. Some chapters seem, on internal evidence, to be considerably older than the 1957 date; oxygen rebreathers for diving and Contax II cameras are obsolete. Many useful hints and much outdoor lore. My favourite quotation is, 'The feeding station idea has endless ramifications . . . carcasses collected along the highways may be placed beneath an attractive perch in an area frequented by vultures . . .'

MILNER, CYRIL DOUGLAS. *The Photography of Scenery* (Focal Press, 1962). Incorporates much of Milner's *Mountain Photography* (1946), now out of print. A lucid and literate book. Specific examples from the author's long experience illuminate his points. Authoritative but not authoritarian. Makes one wish there were books of equal quality on other fields of nature photography.

NESBIT, WILLIAM. *How to Hunt with the Camera; a Complete Guide to All Forms of Outdoor Photography* (New York: E. P. Dutton, 1926). A charming antique; shows how far we have come since 'the late Theodore Roosevelt' and John Burroughs dominated the conservation scene.

ON NATURE IN GENERAL

Standard field guides, such as the Peterson Field Guide Series are indispensable. Another book that has proved to be particularly useful, as well as inspiring, is Rachel Carson's *The Edge of the Sea*, which is available in a pocket-size paperback edition (Mentor Books, and Muller, 1959).

Index: